ELEMENTS OF THE **EXTRAORDINARY**

ESP

Are you a Mind-reader

ELEMENTS OF THE **EXTRAORDINARY**

ESP

Are you a Mind-reader

ANDY BOOT
Illustrated by Terry McKenna

ELEMENT
CHILDREN'S BOOKS

SHAFTESBURY, DORSET · BOSTON, MASSACHUSETTS · MELBOURNE, VICTORIA

© Element Children's Books 1998
Text © Andy Boot 1998
Illustrations © Terry McKenna 1998

First published in Great Britain in 1998 by Element Children's Books
Shaftesbury, Dorset SP7 8BP

Published in the USA in 1998 by Element Books Inc.
PO Box 830, Boston MA

Published in Australia in 1998 by Element Books Limited for Penguin Books
Australia Ltd, 487 Maroondah Highway, Hardbacks, Ringwood, Victoria 3134

All rights reserved. No part of this publication may be reproduced or
transmitted or utilized in any form or by any means, electronic, mechanical,
photocopying or otherwise, without the prior permission of the Publisher.

The moral rights of the author and illustrator have been asserted.

British Library Cataloguing in Publication data available.
Library of Congress Cataloguing in Publication data available.

ISBN 1 901881 25 3

Cover design by Ness Wood
Photography credits: black cat and diviner - courtesy of Jon Stone
Printed and bound in Great Britain by
Creative Print and Design (Wales), Ebbw Vale

Contents

Chapter One: What is ESP? 6

Chapter Two: But is it More Than Just One Thing? 14

Chapter Three: Weird Stuff About Science, Physics, and Why the *X Files* Aren't That Strange 37

Chapter Four: ESP With Animals 54

Chapter Five: Automatic Writing and Ghosts 69

Chapter Six: How Do You Get ESP? 91

Chapter Seven: Yes, But What Can You Do With It? 121

CHAPTER 1

What is ESP?

That's a good question. For a start, what do the letters stand for?

E = extra
S = sensory
P = perception

So ESP is extra sensory perception. That was easy enough ... But hang on, what does it actually mean? After all, it's easy enough to ask someone what ESP means and get an answer like "extra sensory perception," but you still don't know much about it. If you have this thing called ESP, what's going to happen to you? What do you experience? Why is it different from everyday life?

Okay, so there are a lot of questions there. And if you stick with this book from here until the very last page (which, if I can predict the future, will tell you about why earning a living with ESP is almost impossible – now flip to the back and see if my prediction was correct) you'll find out the answers to most of them.

But not all. Because the one totally weird thing about ESP is that everyone knows it exists to some extent – but no one can actually prove it!

Sounds weird, I know, but the reasons for that will make sense later on. For now, let's just talk about what ESP is.

This thing called extra sensory perception means that you can "see," "hear," or "feel" things that aren't actually there. It's as though there are two different worlds: one world is the everyday one that we all live in, where you play computer games, ride your bike, go to school, and do all the things that everyone else does.

The other world is hidden from us. It's a strange world where everything that has ever happened, or ever will happen, is all jumbled up together and you need some kind of map to find your way through it. Your extra sensory perception is both a key and a map.

It's a key because it unlocks the door to this strange world, and lets you inside.

It's a map because it enables you to find your way around and maybe make some sense of what you've found.

ESP is something that we all have locked away in that large part of our brains that we don't use. (Did you know that we only use about one-tenth of our brains, if that? That means you can be a real pea-brain and still be smart!) Something that – in some people – comes out and begins to work.

Wait a minute ... if we use only one-tenth of our brains, then what happens in the other ninety per cent?

The Conscious Mind and the Unconscious Mind

The simple answer is that scientists don't really know. Not yet. But there are some things that we do know. When you're awake, you're conscious. And the thinking you do that enables you to walk, talk, eat, think, and daydream is called the conscious mind.

The rest of your mind is the unconscious mind, which is also called the subconscious mind (mostly because scientists like to confuse people by giving things more than one name). This part of the mind is what makes you dream – all the strange things that you dream about are the result of your subconscious mind combing through everything that is happening in your brain and letting you know about it. It's somewhere in here that ESP is born. In fact, some people who have ESP receive messages about the future from their dreams.

So the subconscious mind is doing all kinds of weird stuff that we can't explain yet. And ESP would seem to be part of that weird stuff breaking through and coming to us when we're conscious.

Some scientists believe in what they call "the information universe." We can't actually see or hear a lot of what happens in the world: some sounds are too high or too low for our ears to receive them, and some rays of light are outside the range of the spectrum that our eyes can see – this includes things like X-rays.

In the same way, some scientists believe that everything that ever happened or ever will happen exists AT THE SAME MOMENT, and what we call time doesn't really exist! We move through all these experiences, and by moving we create time. And as we move, we only see little bits of what's going on, even though everything is there. (More on this strange idea later!)

What ESP does is help us to see a little bit more of what's going on than we usually do. For instance, because what happens today, tomorrow, and yesterday is all there at the same time, people with ESP can catch a glimpse of tomorrow while they're still in today. Somehow, their subconscious mind has noticed tomorrow's events going on around them and has communicated them to their conscious mind.

This difference between being conscious and unconscious

is quite important, because a lot of people with ESP have to go into trances before their ESP will work. Did I mention how many different things can be classed as ESP? Never mind, we'll get to that in a little while. A trance is somewhere between sleeping and waking: in a trance you're neither asleep nor awake. In fact, it's a bit like that feeling you get in the morning when you first wake up and you're all warm and dozy. This trance state seems to act as bridge between the conscious and unconscious mind, enabling any faculty for ESP to jump across from your subconscious mind and come through to you so that you're aware of it.

But for some people, it happens when they're awake, and they notice it in the same way that you or I would notice a dog crossing the road (or a cat, if you prefer them). So it's an extra sense. Sort of.

But extra in what way?

ESP in Relation to the Other Senses

Ordinarily, we have five senses: sight, hearing, touch, taste, and smell. And we have clearly visible parts of the body that can do this sensing for us and transfer the sensations to our brain. Our eyes, ears, fingers, tongues, and noses are easy to see.

The problem with ESP is that there isn't a part of the body you can point to in the same way and say "that's where it comes from."

If you watch old films, or read old books where they talk about ESP, they always call it "sixth sense," as though it were an extra sense to add on to the other five. This is true in as much as it is another way of getting information about the world around us into our conscious mind. But it's also slightly misleading: as you'll see in Chapter Two, the many forms of ESP tend to use the five senses that we already have. Many psychics – people with ESP abilities – tend to see things, hear them, or smell them. Techniques such as dowsing use the senses to channel whatever the ESP has discovered into physical movement – the movement of the dowsing rod. (If you're scratching your head at this point because you don't know what dowsing is, jump ahead to Chapter Two, read it through, then come back. ESP is such a complex subject that you could begin reading about it at any point and still be confused!)

So ESP works with the five senses we have, and also works in addition to them: people who see the future in dreams don't use their five senses (as far as we know), neither do people who are remote viewing (I'll explain this technique in Chapter Two).

It's no wonder scientists have a hard time with ESP!

Why Is It Hard to Pin Down?

Because it isn't merely one thing. As you'll see in Chapter Two (coming up soon), there are several ways in which extra sensory perception can show itself. But it doesn't always do so – people who have ESP will tell you that it happens when it happens, and that it's very hard to make it happen on demand.

The problem is that scientists need it to happen when their experiments are ready. And they need it to be repeated. If you've started doing science at school, you'll know that in order to prove a hypothesis in an experiment, you need to have the same result repeated again and again, just to make sure that the first result wasn't a fluke. But ESP is very erratic, and happens when it feels like it. No one knows why. Unfortunately, this means that very few psychics have been able to go into a laboratory and reproduce their results again and again.

Some psychics, such as Uri Geller, have been able to bend metal under strict laboratory conditions – but not again and again. Others, including Chris Robinson, a man who can predict the future in his dreams, have sometimes been able to get things right under scientific conditions ... but not always.

This makes some scientists believe that ESP doesn't really exist. Others believe that it does, but that they will have to design experiments that take its erratic nature into account. One of these scientists is Professor Arthur Ellison, whom you'll read about in Chapter Three.

So why won't it always work? It could be because ESP comes from the unconscious mind, so if you try too hard to make it work, your conscious mind blocks it out and stops it from breaking through.

The other main problem for scientists who want to prove it exists is that a lot of people have flashes of ESP but never really develop it into a skill. ESP is like riding a bike. You can't become good at it unless you practice!

If you have it in any small way, it comes to you sometimes when you know what someone is going to say before they say it ... When the phone rings and you know who it is even before you answer ...

ESP can be fun, but it may also be scary when it happens to you for the first time. In the chapters that follow, we'll look at the different kinds of ESP, what you can do to develop any talents you may have, and how different people have used their ESP powers.

Sometimes writing about, and reading about, ESP can be confusing. No one is really sure what it is or where it comes from. There is no right or wrong, because all we have are ideas about what MIGHT be happening. So every now and then I'll ask you some questions for which there are no right or wrong answers. They are there to help you think about what you've read, and what seems to make sense to you.

Enjoy the ride.

CHAPTER 2

But is it More Than Just One Thing?

Yes. ESP is something that comes to different people in different ways. No two people who have some kind of ESP will experience it in exactly the same way. Which is something else that makes it very hard to prove. But, generally speaking, there are eight ways in which ESP shows itself.

Telepathy

Or mind-reading. Which is what telepathy is, basically. No one is very sure about how this works, but it seems that some people are able to send their thoughts to other people – to talk to them without actually speaking – either in words or in pictures. And there are people who are able to read thoughts, without the person whose thoughts they are reading even realizing that this is happening.

Two strange things seem to happen to the body when this is going on. First, the patterns of the sender's brainwaves appear to change, as though going on to another frequency, like a radio that's being retuned. Russian scientists discovered this in the early 1980s. And Douglas Dean, a British biologist and physicist, has discovered that when someone is sending his or her thoughts in an ESP test, the blood volume of the sender actually increases – as though the brain were calling for more oxygen from the blood for whatever work it is doing!

Mind-reading on stage has been popular in variety shows for hundreds of years, yet most stage mind-readers don't have any ESP at all. Instead, they have a code with their assistant, so that if the assistant picks up a watch he or she has a way of letting the mind-reader on stage know what he or she is holding. This sort of code and trickery is fun, but has sometimes proved challenging to serious ESP researchers when people taking part in telepathy tests have tried to cheat.

However, strict rules are observed, and scientists tend to do a large number of tests. They compare the number of times a supposedly "psychic" person gets the answer right to those of someone who isn't psychic, in order to work out how much ESP this person has.

HERE ARE SOME TESTS THAT YOU AND A FRIEND COULD TRY:

◆✦ Take a pack of ordinary playing cards. One person decides to be the "sender," one the "receiver." The sender looks at a card without showing it to the receiver, who has to say whether it is red or black. To do this, the sender sits behind the receiver, shuffles the cards, and looks at the face of the first card. Tap the card to let the receiver know you have started, then try to transmit the color of the card mentally.

The best way to do this is either to imagine that the words "red" or "black" are coming out of the middle of your forehead, or to think of something that's the right color – a black dog or a red apple, perhaps. The receiver then has to say what color he or she thinks you are sending.

The sender notes down whether or not the answer was correct. Continue for the whole pack of cards. The law of averages says you should get 26 cards right out of 52. A lot more than this shows a degree of ESP. A lot less also suggests some ESP, because the receiver is somehow blocking the experiment without realizing it.

►► The above experiment can be done exactly as described but by using a set of colored cards. To do this, take several pieces of card in different colors — red, blue, white, green, pink, or whatever you can find. Cut up these pieces of card so you have four of each color — just as you have four suits of playing cards.

Carry out the experiment in exactly the same way as described for the first experiment. See what sort of results you get. Then remove one card of each color, so you only have three of each. Keep doing this until you only have one card of each color, and see if the results remain consistent.

If they do, try this: the sender puts odd numbers of the colors into the pack — say one white, two green, three red, one blue — so that the statistical odds of getting the answer right by guessing are completely thrown. It's interesting to see what kind of result you get when this happens.

◆✦ This third experiment is the classic "circle/square/triangle/wave" experiment, and is a variation on the above. You take four cards, one with a circle drawn on it, one a square, one a triangle, and the last one a series of wavy lines.

Sit as before, and pick one of the four cards at random, shuffling them each time. Try to send the image on the card you pick, noting each time whether the receiver gets the right answer. If the receiver gets more than one-quarter of the answers right, then it shows a good degree of ESP. This is a good experiment to try when you've already started to develop any ESP you may have.

Psychometry

This is the technique in which someone with ESP holds an object – anything from a favorite book to a piece of clothing – and receives impressions about the person who owns it. Many psychics who work with the police to trace missing people use this method to "see" what has happened to them. (There are lots of stories about this later on in the book.)

When the psychic holds the object, he or she doesn't see things as if watching a film, but receives a jumbled impression of pictures, thoughts, sounds, smells, and tastes that he or she has to interpret.

Why does this happen? There are two ideas that may explain it. The first is that objects that are close to a person may act like a kind of video recorder, and retain impressions of what has happened around them. In some way, it seems that the person with ESP is able to act like a TV and plug into this video recorder.

The second idea is that a loved object becomes tuned in to the vibrations of the person it belongs to, and becomes somehow attached to him or her. This might sound weird, but the Buddhist religion has claimed that a human being is a set of vibrations that have to be in harmony with their surroundings, and science shows us that we are all collections of atoms that vibrate at different frequencies, all vibrating together to form solid matter. (What a thought!) So if we use something a lot, perhaps it absorbs part of us and becomes tuned to our own personal vibrations.

HERE'S A PSYCHOMETRY EXPERIMENT YOU CAN TRY:

For this you need an object from someone that you don't know very well – say your friend's mum or dad. Hold it and concentrate on it. See what comes into your head, and write it down. Then ask your friend's mum or dad to read what you've written and see if it means anything to them. You may be surprised at what you come up with – and so might they!

It's very important that you have an object from someone you don't know very well, because then there's no possibility of your writing down something that you already know.

Dowsing

Dowsing is a technique where you search for something using either a rod or a pendulum. What this object seems to do is to tap into energies that are outside the body and feed them into your mind. The two types of dowsing are quite different, and we'll look at them separately.

RODS

Most people know about dowsing rods because they are used to search for water, but they can also be used to hunt for a number of other things in the earth.

It seems that, when held loosely in the hand, the rods – two pieces of metal, or a hazel twig (which is a favorite tool of water-diviners) – can be used as antennae, reacting to whatever you are thinking about.

The best way to try this is to make your own rods from a couple of wire coat-hangers. Cut up each one so that you have a long rod with a short handle. Make sure you file off any rough pieces of metal so that you don't cut yourself. Balance a rod loosely in each hand, so that you're not holding them still but are not making them move voluntarily either. Then ask someone to bury something in the garden – make sure you don't know where they've dug. If you walk around the garden, thinking about the object, you may find that the rods respond by crossing at a certain spot – and that spot may be where the object is buried!

You can then try this again with such things as water pipes – many people are very successful when dowsing for water. But don't start digging up the water pipes, or your mum and dad might have some angry visitors from the water company!

If you do not have a garden, or don't fancy the idea of digging around in the mud, you could ask someone to hide something in a room in your house (but make sure you are not standing there when they do it!) and then try to find the object using your dowsing rods. This experiment can also be carried out with the pendulum, which brings us nicely to…

PENDULUMS

A pendulum is suspended from a piece of string, and it can be made of wood or metal, or can even be a crystal. Very often, pendulums are crystals, and you can buy these easily. The pendulum is like a finely-tuned rod because it works in the same way, but it gives much more precise results. Once again, it seems that the pendulum filters information into your brain and acts as a focus for ESP. Whereas the rods will cross when they find what you are looking for, the pendulum spins, either clockwise or counterclockwise. One way means "yes," the other means "no." It's up to you to find out which is which, because everyone's pendulums work differently. So the first thing to do is to think of a few questions to which you already know the answers. For instance, in order to "prime" my pendulum and know which way it spins when it says "yes", I ask it "Is my name Andy Boot?" I see if it spins in a clockwise or counterclockwise direction, and then ask a question to which the correct answer is "no." So if I ask "Is my cat Tooty ten years old?" I watch for the "no" response (because he's eighteen). I repeat the experiment with a few more questions until I'm absolutely sure which way is "yes" and which is "no."

The pendulum can then be used to discover a lot of things. Tom Lethbridge, a retired professor about whom you'll read more in Chapter Three, found the pendulum by accident and became fascinated by it. He conducted many experiments and found that a lot of objects have their own "vibration" to which the pendulum will respond. For instance, he found that, when placed over silver, the pendulum would spin 22 times – but only if the length of string on the pendulum was 22in (56cm)!

Findings like these have been invaluable to people like Uri Geller. He will set the pendulum length for whatever he is searching for – say silver – and hold the pendulum over maps of the areas where mining is to take place, thinking all the time of silver. When the pendulum starts to spin, he will mark that spot on the map.

Psychics have also used this method to locate missing people. With a pendulum set over a map of an area where someone disappeared, and by thinking of him or her, the psychic has sometimes been able to trace the route that the missing person took by noting where the pendulum starts to spin.

You can begin your own experiments with a pendulum almost immediately. As soon as you get your own pendulum, prime it using the method described above.

If you have a pet, hold the pendulum over the pet and

think of what kind of animal it is. If the pendulum starts to spin, note which way it is moving and the length of the string. This may change with each item, so using a pendulum can be quite frustrating at first. Unlike with the rods, it takes quite a lot of trial and error to get a pendulum working properly.

But if you persevere it can be really worthwhile, because you will start to find the rates of spin and string length for lots of things. You will be able to find things on maps and also to search for lost pets by thinking of them and trying to follow a route shown by the swinging pendulum.

And there's a lot more besides to pendulums, as you'll see when we start talking about Tom Lethbridge in Chapter Three.

Psychokinesis

This long word means the ability to make things happen to objects through the power of ESP. No one can even begin to explain how this happens, and there is little in the way of home experiment that you can try to see whether or not you can do this. Which is perhaps just as well! For instance, would your mum be very pleased if she came home to find that you'd been holding all the knives and forks in the house and making them bend, as Uri Geller can do? He does this simply by concentrating on the image of the metal bending! He can make clocks stop or start by looking at them.

There are some people, such as the American Ted Serios, who can make images appear on camera film. He became celebrated in the 1960s for putting an unexposed and undeveloped film in the camera and, by holding the camera and concentrating very hard, making the emulsion on the film change in such a way as to form a picture. Other people have been able to levitate tables, and even themselves, simply by the power of thought. A lot of discipline is involved in this, and there is even a spiritual path called transcendental meditation which, if you get really good at it, can help you to levitate.

Psychokinesis can also be used to make a glass move on a table so that it will point to a card or an object that you are thinking about very hard. This is not the sort of thing you can try if you are just starting to discover if you have any ESP, because it requires so much mind-power. Even the people who can do this usually need to practice for a very long time before it will work for them!

But it is possible to do really amazing things with psychokinesis. For instance, Suzanne Padfield – whom you'll read more about later – was able to make a beam of light bend when she was experimenting in Benson Herbert's laboratory in the south of England. And the American, Ingo Swann, was able to affect the electronic temperature-register in a laboratory, so that the reading changed even though the temperature did not. Even more amazing, he managed to alter the reading on a magnetometer, a sensitive piece of electronic equipment that was shielded by a lead screen – something that even X-rays can't penetrate!

Ingo Swann was also involved in the next display of ESP skill ...

Remote Viewing

The Stanford Research Institute is in California, and it was after a series of tests in the 1970s, many of which featured Ingo Swann, that the researchers coined the term "remote viewing" for a kind of ESP that is best described as long-distance telepathy.

It worked like this: the scientists involved, Russell Targ

But is it More Than Just One Thing? • 27

and Harold Puthoff, had a series of envelopes on which were written map co-ordinates. The psychics were then put into a room and given a collection of maps. An envelope was picked at random, and its map co-ordinates were read out to the psychics. They would then find this exact location on the relevant map, and relax ...

They would then write down and draw the impressions they were getting, and these would be checked against what was actually at this point on the map.

What did they see in their minds? One map co-ordinate turned out to be of a famous landmark on the Stanford Campus called the Hoover Tower. A psychic, Pat Price, who had just flown into Stanford and had never seen the town before, not only described and drew the tower but was also able to name it!

The US Government later took over the project and used it for spying purposes – as you'll find out later in this book. But meanwhile, how about a bit of DIY remote viewing?

Obviously, you won't be able to do this with maps from all around the world (unless you know someone who lives in the country that you choose), but you can try it with a relative or friend who lives some way away from you. Ask him or her to send you a map of the town or village and a series of sealed envelopes with map co-ordinates written on them. Get your mum or dad to pick one at random, and find the spot on the map that corresponds with these co-ordinates.

Relax, and see what comes into your mind when you think about that spot. Write down and draw what you see. Then send a copy of your writing and drawing to whoever supplied the map. Ask your friend or relative to tell you if you've got anything right. Ask him or her to take photographs of that location so you can compare it with what you have written or drawn.

And keep repeating the experiment! Practice is everything in developing whatever skills you may have, so don't give up if your results aren't great at first.

Clairvoyance and Clairaudience

These are the most famous and well-known forms of ESP, and are usually associated with ghosts. That's because people who are clairvoyant or clairaudient can see or hear ghosts. What we call ghosts aren't necessarily the spirits of people who have died, as we'll see later on. They may be the form in which some psychics can see and hear information that is passed through their unconscious minds. To them the information appears as a ghost, whereas to someone else it will appear as a vision or vivid image.

Clairvoyants actually see ghosts. They can see people in front of them who talk to them and tell them things, or who merely do the same thing over and over again. (These are the two types of ghost that can be seen – skip to the section on ghosts right now if you can't wait to find out more, then get back here quick!)

Clairaudients hear voices. They won't actually see a ghost as such, but they will hear people talking to them and telling them things. Both words – "clairvoyant" and "clairaudient" – come from the French and basically mean someone who sees and someone who hears clearly.

One of the most famous clairaudients was a British psychic called Doris Stokes, who used to appear in big concert halls around the world and tell people what she could hear – often voices that seemed to belong to relatives or friends of people in the audience.

I once went to see a clairvoyant called Keith Hudson, who lived in East London, near where I lived at the time. He had a bookshop that I used to go into, and was a very down-to-earth man – we both liked detective stories and would talk about them for ages. But Keith also appeared at the local Spiritualist church (Spiritualists are Christians who believe that everyone in heaven can talk to us through people who have ESP), and I went to see him. It was quite fascinating, because he acted as though ghosts were standing next to him talking to him – sometimes he'd have to shut them up if they wouldn't let him finish what he was saying to the people in the church!

Whatever Keith was getting via his ESP – whether it was ghosts or something else – he believed in it, and he certainly said a lot of things that made sense to people he didn't know in the audience.

There are also people who can smell things, or even taste them – a scientist called Gustav Pagenstecher once tested a psychic who could taste the food that Gustav was eating!

There are no real experiments I would suggest you try for this – it's something that just happens to you if you have ESP, and it's perhaps something that you need to be ready for in your own time. It can be quite frightening if you're not!

However, if you feel that you do have some kind of ESP, and you feel confident and happy enough to try it, then there is something you could do to practice with your ESP...

The first thing to do is to find a house or place that is known to be haunted. There are always lots of houses and buildings that are supposed to have ghosts, and most libraries have books that are guides to haunted houses. Your local paper might also be a good bet – they always love true-life ghost stories. However, don't read too much information about the place before you visit it, otherwise your imagination could play tricks on you. Leave the reading for afterwards ...

When you've found somewhere and travelled to it, just walk around and see what you can feel and sense. Most old houses that are open to the public have some sort of legend connected with ghosts. Make a record of what you feel and see, and then compare these impressions with the stories about that place and its history. Check if you "saw" anything that has been described elsewhere.

Dream Precognition

This is something you can try, and I'll tell you how in a little while. But first of all, what is it? Well, precognition means that you get a glimpse of the future. It's called dream precognition because it usually happens in the form of a dream while you are asleep. Not always, though – some people can see glimpses of the future while they are awake, and then it's almost like a day-dream.

Some dream precognition is very straightforward. For instance, a newspaper editor called W.T. Stead once dreamed that he was on a giant ship and that it sank. This made such an impact on him that he wrote about his remarkable dream – but it didn't stop him from booking a passage to New York on the biggest liner in the world when it was launched in 1912. That ship was the *Titanic*, and Stead was one of the hundreds who drowned when it struck an iceberg and sank.

In Chapter Three you'll read all about a man called J.W. Dunne, who started to write down all his dreams and became convinced that everyone has premonitions of the future in their dreams. The problem is that most people forget their dreams! He wrote a book about his ideas, and claimed that dreaming is a way in which we travel in time.

How can we see the future in our dreams? There are some scientific theories, and Tom Lethbridge had a few interesting notions after some of his pendulum experiments. He thought that time as we know it doesn't exist outside the physical world – and the odd thing is that this ties in with a lot of ideas in very old religions. Even relatively modern ones, such as Christianity which is only 2,000 years old (a youngster compared with Islam and Buddhism!), seem to teach this – after all, no one ever gets old in heaven.

In Chapter Three we'll discuss these ideas about time, and the exploits of Dunne and Lethbridge. But there are other notions about dream precognition that need to be looked at.

I once wrote a book about a psychic called Chris Robinson, who has dreams that come true. He has dreamed about IRA bombers and has helped the police as a result.

He's also dreamed about all sorts of news stories and trivial everyday things – he once dreamed that his car overheated on a road and he had to park behind a woman in a Peugeot. Three days later, this happened while I was with him! And I'd already seen the piece of paper on which he scribbled his dream!

Chris believes that all people can see the future in dreams, but not only do they forget easily (he sleeps so lightly that he actually writes in his sleep or when half-awake), they don't realize that their dreams mean anything because they dream in symbols. For instance, when Chris dreams about the IRA they appear as dogs because he's frightened of dogs. And when it snows in his dreams, he knows that something nasty is going to happen. Sometimes it's an obvious dream but a lot of the time he dreams in this strange code, and it took him some time to work out what it all meant.

So, if you want to know if you can tell the future in your dreams, this might be the best way to go about it ...

The first thing to do is to write down all you can remember about your dreams every morning as soon as you wake up. Make sure you write down every detail. And don't be surprised or disappointed if things don't make sense at first.

Don't worry if nothing happens for a few days – the average length of time between a dream and anything in it actually taking place is three days, although some things may take ages.

As soon as something happens that you think you dreamed about, look in your dream diary and see how you described the dream. Is there anything that didn't make sense at the time but which now seems more obvious? In Chris's case, he noticed that he always dreamed about dogs when there was an IRA incident. So he worked out that dogs symbolized the IRA. Maybe you dream in symbols too?

Keep a record of anything that seems to come true, and when. It will take a bit of time, but if you do have any kind of ESP that works through dream precognition then you'll gradually build up a list of dreams that have come true, a list of those that haven't, and a list of what the symbols in your dreams mean in real life.

There is no right or wrong to this – it's something that is individual to you, and that you'll only be able to discover for yourself. So dream on!

Who Are These People We Call Psychics?

That's a good question, because I use the terms "psychic" and "medium" quite a lot in this book.

"Psychic" is a term that comes from the idea that people have psi power – that is, something that science cannot quite explain yet which cannot be denied. ESP is also called psi.

"Medium" is related to the word "media" – just as information is used in the media of television and books, so a person with psi power is a medium for information that comes from the unconscious. It's an old term that was used in the early days of psychic research, and is not used quite so much these days.

But what is it that makes these people different? What is it that enables them to have this power? And do you or I have it?

The answer is that, as with everything else involved with ESP, no one knows for sure. One school of thought says that we are on the verge of a big leap forward in evolution, where we will use more of our brains than we currently do (remember that we only use ten percent of them at the moment), and that psychics are the first examples of that leap forward. One day, we'll all be like them.

The other school of thought is that there is something in their bodies that enables their minds to break through one part of their brain to another. Michael Bentine, the comedian whose father was a scientist studying psychics (and I predict you'll read some AMAZING things about him in Chapter Five!), pointed out that a psychic who got good results one moment might not after having a cup of tea or getting excited. This is because the tea changed the chemical balance of the body, and getting excited released adrenaline, which also changed the body's chemistry. Moving on from this, some scientists believe that people with certain blood types, or who are a certain body shape, or who eat certain kinds of food, are more likely to be psychics.

We are still in the early days of this sort of research, and results are still very confusing, but perhaps one day we'll be able to train our bodies to help our brains to develop ESP!

CHAPTER 3

Weird Stuff About Science, Physics, and Why the X Files Aren't That Strange

If you think that Fox Mulder has some wacko ideas, wait until you read the theories of some scientists and researchers on why ESP happens!

In this chapter, you're going to read about Buddhism and Christianity put next to Paganism, and also about the idea of different planes of existence that work as spirals where time doesn't exist AS WE KNOW IT! Also about why we're walking across a gigantic dining table.

Yeah, that bit DOES look weird. Read on – you'll never get Mulder and Scully walking across a massive dinner table...

First of all, we need to look at what the physical and spiritual universe means. Ever since the apple dropped on Isaac Newton's head and he discovered the law of gravity (well, it had always existed, but he suddenly realized what it was when no one else had yet caught on), science has believed in what it calls the mechanical universe. This means that everything you can touch, feel, and see is real, and if you can't prove it in this manner it does not exist. As you might have guessed, conventional scientists don't like the idea of ESP because it can't be proved.

On the other side of the fence to the scientists and their universe that runs like clockwork are the people who follow various religious and spiritual paths. Take Paganism, for instance – this is a term that covers a lot of spiritual beliefs that go way back in time, beyond religions that are long-established. Many of these beliefs claimed that life on earth was just the start, and that when people died they moved on to another form of existence. There were "spirits" and strange forces without bodies that could exist. There was also the belief that "magic" was something with which to influence other people and the world around you – to make something change simply by wishing it, really.

Other spiritual paths evolved into the religions we know today. Christians believe in a heaven and hell, where people go when they die – in other words, there is some part of us that isn't only physical, but that can survive without a body. Buddhists believe that something called "karma" exists. It's hard to describe their complex beliefs simply, in a few sentences, but basically they feel that this life is a training ground for something that comes next. We all have a soul, and it is part of the big pool of souls from which we all come, and to which we all return. Karma is a kind of profit and loss account that we build up in our life, and if we don't seem to have learned much in this life then our soul will come back again and again in different forms until we have learned. What are we supposed to be learning? I'm not sure – which probably means that I'm due to come back again!

One of the interesting things about these ideas is that they all seem to work on the assumption that we move up a scale – whether it's what are called planes of existence (ever heard the phrase "the astral plane?" It's the next one up from the physical, and is where we lose our bodies), or spirals of existence that we work our way up, like swimming the wrong way up a waterspout!

There didn't seem to be any way that these ideas and those of science would meet. But then came ...

The Wacky World of Quantum Physics

Physicists had always assumed that the atom was the smallest possible object in the universe, and could not be split any further. Then they discovered atomic power, which comes from splitting the atom in two. Around the same time, they discovered that, far from being a single entity, the atom was actually made up of smaller things – electrons and neutrons.

Then it started to get really, really weird. Scientists who had devised a way of watching these things that made up atoms discovered that they were doing two very bizarre things. First, the scientists were firing electrons at mesh with really, REALLY small holes, to see how they behaved. Some would go through the mesh as a wave, and some as a particle. So the scientists figured that there were two types of electron. Then they looked again, and found that one electron could go through the mesh as a particle and as a wave AT THE SAME TIME!

As if that wasn't strange enough, they then discovered that these electrons acted differently if they weren't watched! They called this the "experimenter" effect.

The earliest discoverer of what we now call quantum physics was Arthur Eddington. He was a young scientist at a time when an old physicist called Sir Oliver Lodge was being laughed at by other scientists over his ideas about Spiritualism. Sir Oliver had lost his son, Raymond, in World War I, and had turned to Spiritualism because he was desperate to know if Raymond's "spirit" had survived death. He wrote several books about his experiences with Spiritualists, and was convinced that he had spoken to Raymond.

Sir Oliver was extremely interested in all ESP and psychic phenomena after this, and he thought Arthur Eddington's findings were fascinating. If it were true that looking at an experiment could in some way change the result, then what were ESP phenomena like levitating tables or bending metal if not the same thing, the same use of mind-power, on a much, much bigger scale?

Even more interesting are the findings of scientists who have come later, including Professor Stephen Hawking.

They believe that space and time are not separate but the same thing – and that everything has already happened and is happening at the same time. According to them, it's only the way that we look at time that makes one day appear to happen after another.

Don't worry if this is all rather confusing – it probably will be for a long time to come! The problem is that these ideas are changing the way we look at the world, and each time we change that perspective we find something else to make us look at things in an even newer way.

Stephen Hawking believes that we see time run in one direction because decay has to build up in the universe. Here's an example: you knock a cup off a table and it hits the floor and breaks. In the timeless universe that exists in the scientists' theory, the cup is on the table, falling, and broken – all at the same time. But because the universe only allows decay and breakage (which the scientists call "entropy") to build up, then we have to see it going one way instead of all ways. The universe simply won't allow breakages to run backwards!

This is really interesting when considering ideas about ESP, because it says that everything is there at the same time. So maybe someone with ESP has a part of the brain that can reach outside the physical world we see and have a look at everything else that is happening before passing this knowledge through to the conscious mind.

Oh No - Not Math!

Oh yes – I'm afraid so.

You see, however much you hate math and however little it may seem to be linked with ESP, it really has quite an important connection.

For instance, most of the complicated ideas in quantum physics are concerned with things that are either too small to be properly seen (did you know that physicists now believe in the existence of things even SMALLER than electrons?) or things that happened so long ago that we can't trace them. So the only way to work out what could have happened is by using the sort of mathematical formulae and algebra that make anything you do in school seem like $1 + 1 = 2$! For instance, the current belief is that the universe began with a big bang, from one single piece of incredibly dense matter. But what came before that?

Scientists think it was things called fields ... but they're not too sure yet what these fields actually were!

Which all seems to have very little to do with ESP – except for the fact that a proof of quantum theory would make it possible for even the most skeptical scientist to admit that the non-physical things that happen in ESP are possible. After all, if you can change an experiment simply by looking at it ...

But never mind all that – math is necessary even in the down-to-earth manner of conducting experiments with psychics. As Professor Arthur Ellison knows.

Ellison is a scientist who has long believed in psychic phenomena. In fact, he belongs to a body called the Society for Psychical Research, which has been in existence since the end of the nineteenth century. As a scientist, Ellison is only too well aware that what scientists like is repeated proof of any theory. Remember how the key to any scientific result is continued proof? Well, Ellison has set about getting exactly that. And what a long, dull business it is, because it involves a form of math called statistics.

What Ellison is doing is this: he has a series of experiments, like some of those you might have tried in Chapter Two, and he conducts test after test after test with some subjects who have ESP and some who don't. He then repeats these tests in different conditions in order to judge the experimenter effect, and the effect of different times of day, different room temperatures, and just about any other difference that you would care to mention.

All these results are logged and tabled, and from them are calculated the results of those people with ESP compared to those people without it. The aim of this is to show disbelievers how those with ESP perform in all kinds of conditions compared to those who don't, and to prove by the difference in figures that such a phenomenon as ESP does exist.

It's funny to think that the final proof accepted by scientists that ESP exists may come from a set of complicated figures rather than an amazing feat of telepathy or psychokinesis!

Tom Lethbridge and His Pendulums

Tom was just as methodical as Arthur Ellison, but in his own way ...

Tom Lethbridge was a professor at Cambridge, England, for many years, and the keeper of the town's archaeological museum. He'd written a few books about myths and legends, and in 1958 decided to retire early and move to Cornwall, where his wife Mina had been born.

When he was a young undergraduate, Tom had a strange experience at Cambridge. In a college chapel, he suddenly walked into a patch of cold, dank air that made him feel very depressed. Although he never thought of it as a ghost as such, he did wonder if there was some way in which an impression of emotions or atmospheres could imprint themselves on the world. It was an idea that came back to him very quickly when he was in Cornwall, because he started to see a ghost by a stream near his new home. He noted that it always did the same thing and, from asking questions, realized that many ghosts seem to occur near running water, or where there is a strong electrical field. If you're intrigued, flick to the chapter on ghosts, where all these ideas are explored. But if you want to stick with Tom, then read on ...

The concept of electrical and magnetic currents being involved with ghosts linked up with Tom's ideas about water divining. So he became interested in dowsing and began a series of experiments with a pendulum, which was the dowsing method shown to him by an old woman.

This was where things started to become really wild. In the chapter on dowsing, we talked about Tom's discoveries concerning the length of the pendulum's string, and how many times it would rotate. But he got beyond that ...

The first strange thing that happened was that, when he thought about death, the pendulum rate was 40 – 40 spins and 40in (102cm) of string. But after that, everything would respond to its pendulum length PLUS the 40in, so silver would respond to 62 turns at 62in (157cm) as well as 22 turns at 22in (56cm)! And – here's the weird bit – the only thing that didn't respond was time! It was as though time didn't exist after the 40in – or after death.

Intrigued, he continued with VERY LONG string and found that it all changed again after another 40in – by this time, Mina was observing the pendulum because the string was so long that Tom was having to do things like hold it out of an upstairs window!

After months of these experiments, Tom evolved a theory. It seemed to him that we follow a kind of spiral, and at each turn there is a cut-off point before it all begins again — as though we go up through the different planes of existence, where everything still exists, but at a different rate of spin or vibration. But time as we know it only exists in this physical world — after all, he could find pendulum rates for everything except time.

So if his unconscious could tap into this with the pendulum, then why not in other ways? Tom began to study his dreams, and noted that there were several incidents in them that seemed to relate to future events. He had the idea that the unconscious mind could see things on other spirals, where time did not exist and the mind could roam free.

Sadly, Tom died in 1971 at the age of 70, and didn't get the chance to finish his experiments. Maybe he now knows for certain about the spirals he described. One thing's for sure, his ideas have inspired other people to research in this area, and they have opened up a whole new world of possibilities.

The Strange Story of J.W. Dunne

Just as Tom Lethbridge discovered that parts of his dreams foretold the future, J.W. Dunne had similar experiences over 40 years before, and was convinced that he could teach everyone to develop ESP powers.

John Dunne trained as an engineer, and in 1914 he dreamed about a train crash that subsequently happened. He found this rather strange, but didn't really think much about it at the time. It was only after a number of smaller premonitions had come true that he began to give the matter some thought. He began to write down as much of his dreams as he could remember, and to keep a note of anything that came true. Then, being trained as an engineer, he tried to work out some kind of system that could account for these happenings.

The result was his 1927 book *An Experiment with Time*, the first half of which was a diary of his experiences and a manual on recording your dreams, and the second half of which was full of mathematical formulae that attempted to prove that the unconscious mind could leap distances in time and see what was happening. Dunne's theory was that time works like the loops on a rollercoaster, and when you are at the top of one, the mind can leap across to the top of the next loop while your body has to go down and then up, taking the long route.

Later discoveries about the universe show us that Dunne probably wasn't right about this, although his ideas were very good for the time in which they were written (science has moved so fast in the twentieth century). What was really remarkable was the response to Dunne's book.

It was a runaway best-seller, and hundreds of thousands of people bought copies, intrigued by the idea that they might be able to foretell the future. Millions more read about it in the British newspaper, the *Daily Express*, which ran a series of articles based on the book. But more than that: Dunne and the *Express* got together to conduct an amazing experiment. Readers across the country were invited to record their dreams and send them in. They would then write in if any of their dreams had come true, and staff on the paper would compare the two accounts to see if the dream really did match the result. Dunne oversaw the whole experiment.

It was an incredible thing for a newspaper to do, because

it took so many staff to collect together the hundreds of thousands of letters that arrived.

At first, it looked as though Dunne would get some interesting results, but as time went on it seemed that people lost interest and their dreams weren't followed up. Sometimes, people sent in the results after forgetting to send in their dreams!

So the whole thing fizzled out. There wasn't enough paperwork for a real conclusion (math again!), but Dunne was satisfied. As far as he was concerned, he had shown people that dream precognition was possible for anyone.

Even if Dunne's idea of the rollercoaster of time wasn't quite right, he was on the right track (bet your ESP didn't see that bad joke coming). That's because there is a theory of time that could explain a lot of ESP ability with dreams and psychometry.

But first – how NOT to make money on horseracing!

Wilbur Wright's Racehorses

No, he's not Orville's brother and the first man to get a plane off the ground, but another Wilbur Wright. He went on a plane of another kind, if you believe that the unconscious mind can move above the physical world.

Wilbur is an English writer, and he was only vaguely aware of Dunne when something odd happened to him. This was 20 years after Dunne's book, and Wilbur could only vaguely remember the fuss it caused when he was a boy.

Three times Wilbur dreamed about a big horserace – not

always the same one, but the Grand National, or the Oaks, or the Cheltenham Cup. Once was in 1946, the second time in 1948. Each time the same thing happened. Wilbur – who wasn't actually interested in racing – dreamed that he was standing on a racecourse when a man approached him. He wore a long coat, binoculars, and a hat. He looked familiar, but frustratingly Wilbur was never able to describe the man to his satisfaction. The man would exchange a few words with him, then give him the name of a horse. Both times the horse won the next day's big race. Wilbur didn't place a bet on either race.

The third time it happened was in 1954. Wilbur was staying with some friends named Cheesewright. The dream happened exactly as before. But this time, when the man approached, Wilbur recognized him and said: 'Oh no, not you again!' The man frowned and looked quite annoyed at being greeted this way. He told Wilbur the name of a horse, raised his hat, and then walked away.

The next day, Wilbur told the Cheesewrights about his dream, and how it had happened before. Mrs Cheesewright placed a bet on the horse and won £100 – which was a lot of money in 1954! Wilbur won nothing – because once again he didn't bet.

The odd thing is that the man never turned up again in Wilbur's dreams. Wilbur suspects that his unconscious mind, feeding him information in a way he could understand, was miffed when he refused to act on it and quite simply refused to give him any more winners!

So how come Wilbur's unconscious could leap about in time? And what does this have to do with the dinner table I mentioned at the start of this chapter?

Time for Universal Dinner

Herman Minkowski was a scientist who had a radical theory. He believed that as well as the three dimensions we have about us, there is a fourth. And if you were to enter that fourth dimension, you would look down on space-time and see that it isn't moving but is static. Everything that has ever happened and ever will happen is all there. Not moving.

The psychic researcher H.T. Saltmarsh thought this theory was very interesting, and wondered if we weren't like tiny insects moving across a dinner table. He explained it like this: suppose the whole universe was like a dinner table, laid out for a meal. All the cutlery, salt and pepper, everything, is already in place. And we – human beings – are like little insects that are walking across the table in a straight line. We only know the salt and pepper are there when we reach them and they come into our field of vision – even though they've been there all the time.

He developed this idea further. If we are walking in a straight line, then our conscious mind is like a very bright, narrowly focused beam of light, seeing only what is directly ahead. But what if our unconscious mind is like a lantern, with a weaker beam of light that spreads out all around? Then we can see far ahead, to the sides, and behind us. We can see more, but not as well as nearer objects. Supposing that both lights are working at the same time, then is it not possible that sometimes we'll catch a glimpse of the future in the weaker beam – in other words, when our unconscious has an opportunity to barge its way into our conscious mind?

H.T. Saltmarsh's idea was simply this: we move through time and only see a very small part of what is going on. Our unconscious can see more but, because it is the weaker beam, we don't notice it as much.

So does this mean that everything that is going to happen is set in stone, and there's nothing we can do to change it? Not necessarily. Some scientists believe in what they call the multiple branching universe, which means that at every point where someone has to make a decision, there are two branches of what happens next, and then two more at the next point – so that the universe of space-time is like a giant spider's web of events! And this may be why psychics are sometimes right and sometimes not – they can see the future, but it might not necessarily be the future we move in!

Enough of this confusing science! All these ideas show us why ESP is possible, and how some people seek to explain it. But until it's proved, the only thing we really have to show for it are our own experiences when we try it, and the amazing stories of people to whom ESP events happen.

So let's get away from the scientists and look at some more strange happenings ...

CHAPTER 4

ESP With Animals

Strange as it may seem, animals seem to have more ESP than many humans. Lots of psychologists, scientists and so-called experts (which is what I'm supposed to be – but I'll let you into a little secret: no one is really an expert on things like ESP, because we don't know enough about it yet!) have huge and massive arguments about whether or not animals have psychic powers.

This isn't surprising. Lots of priests used to argue about whether or not animals had souls. And still no one can prove it or disprove it.

The argument about animals having ESP has one set of scientists lining up and shouting about how animals can't possibly have ESP because they aren't intelligent enough. The other set of scientists, who disagree, shout just as loudly that the first set of scientists are right about animals not having as much intelligence as human beings – and say that's precisely why they're wrong about them not having ESP. These scientists claim that because animals don't have as much of an operating conscious mind as human beings, they have less to obstruct the natural flow of ESP power from other parts of their brains.

What do I think? I think that neither side can actually prove what they're saying as yet – but I'm pretty sure that some animals do have ESP in the same way as some humans.

My own experience of this is with my cat, Tooty. He's a very old man, now, because he's 18. He's a bit frail and has trouble using the cat flap, which means that he sometimes can't open it very easily. So he wants me to let him in.

How do I know he wants that? Because sometimes, even when I don't know that he's out, I suddenly get the feeling that I know he's out there. And when I go to look, there he is, looking pleased with himself because he can come back in without having to struggle with the cat flap. There have even been times when I've been really hard up, waiting for a check to arrive (being a writer means you have anxious mornings waiting for the postman to call), and I've complained to Tooty that I really need some money. The next day something happens – I get a check in the mail, or someone phones up to offer me work.

Don't even ask me how he does that!

Van Osten's Mind-reading Horses

But what has this got to do with Van Osten's horses? And who was he?

Wilhelm Van Osten was a Prussian aristocrat who lived in the second half of the nineteenth century. Prussia was a tiny part of what is now Germany, and like all the aristocracy in Prussia Van Osten was very interested in horses. One of his hobbies was to breed and train them. One of the tricks he wanted to teach his horses was how to read numbers off a card. They would be shown a card, and would then stamp their hooves to indicate the number on the card.

Okay, it might seem slightly crazy to want to teach horses to count, but Van Osten was like that. Which is just as well, as otherwise he wouldn't have spotted that something very odd happened when his horses were counting. Sometimes he would look at the card before he showed it to the horses, and sometimes he would simply hold it up. Sometimes the horses stamped the right number of times, and sometimes they didn't. Van Osten found this extremely frustrating, until he realized that the horses got the number correct when he showed them a card that he had looked at first!

He thought that perhaps the horses were able to read his mind. He got very excited by this and decided to put his mind-reading horses on display. A number of scientists studied him, including the part-time fairy tale writer Maurice Maeterlinck (more on him later). They realized that the horses weren't so much reading Van Osten's mind as interpreting a series of very slight twitches and spasms in his face as he tried to think very hard about the number – each number had its own special set of twitches!

So did this mean that Van Osten's horses weren't reading

his mind? Well, they were in a way – his mind made his face twitch minutely, and the horses were translating this into a number.

It was many years before a scientist called Roger Sperry linked the twitches to strange goings-on in different parts of the brain ...

Have Fun With Two Brains

As you'll see later, "ghosts" tend to appear where there is some form of electro-magnetic field (which is where the lines of power in the earth create electric and magnetic currents that run very strongly). If you're intrigued, skip to that bit, but come back as soon as you've read it, because ...

We're going to talk about how the physical and the mental come together. After all, you can't live without your body in the physical world, and your body can't function without the mental powers and electrical pulses of your brain. The two go together and work in harmony.

This is how many scientists think dowsing works. The muscles of the body receive signals from the brain, affected by the electro-magnetic currents of the earth, that make the dowser's muscles twitch and therefore make either the pendulum or the divining rod move in a certain way. These are the same kind of twitches that Van Osten's horses were reading.

Roger Sperry was a scientist who was interested in how the brain works. He was introduced to a man with a head injury that meant the two halves of his brain were no longer connected. This was interesting to Sperry, because the left side of the brain generally governs our ordinary actions, such as moving, talking, and thinking about everyday tasks. The right-hand side of the brain, on the other hand (or brain!), does its fair share of the everyday stuff – after all, the left side of the body is governed by the right side of the brain – but is generally the part that deals with being creative and with dreaming: the part that we call the unconscious or subconscious mind.

Sperry wanted to test the theory that we're all so concerned with the everyday stuff that we've lost touch with the right-hand side of the brain, and so miss all the things that animals can still experience – such as the electromagnetic currents that dowsers can feel, or that birds use to fly vast distances without a map and still know where they're going. (Which is just as well, since birds don't have a spare wing to hold any maps while they fly!)

Sperry covered the man's right eye (which went into the left brain) and flashed red and green lights into his left eye – which was, if you remember, unconnected to his severed right brain.

Sperry then asked the man what the colors were. He noted that when the man couldn't answer – because the signals from his eye hadn't reached his left brain or been relayed from the unconnected right brain – his face was contorted by twitches and muscle spasms, as though his body were trying to force the message across the gap.

From this, Sperry decided that the twitches that were

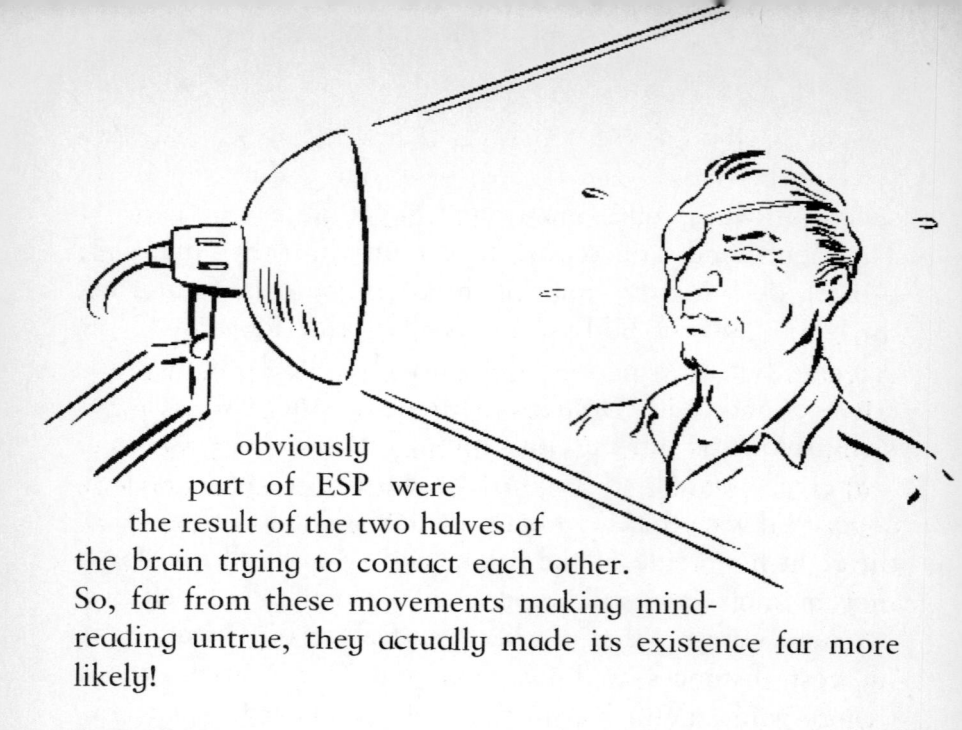

obviously part of ESP were the result of the two halves of the brain trying to contact each other. So, far from these movements making mind-reading untrue, they actually made its existence far more likely!

QUESTIONS

- ◆ Do you think all ESP is a result of seeing things like facial twitches and reading them without actually realizing that you're doing it?
- ◆ If you do, then how is it that people have ESP experiences in dreams?

Maurice Maeterlinck and ESP

Maurice Maeterlinck was a Belgian who lived in many parts of Europe, and who was an immensely popular writer in the first few decades of the twentieth century. One of his most famous books was a collection of fairy stories called *The Bluebird*. The title story has been made into a film several times, and is a funny little tale about a bluebird who is searching for a great treasure and enlists the help of animals and humans who join him in his hunt. They are all able to communicate with each other without talking, and overcome all their differences in the hunt for the treasure.

Really, this fable isn't about a treasure hunt — it's more about what the animals and humans learn along the way. And that's all about nature being stronger than any one species, and how they can all get along if they give in to nature and learn from it. That's how they begin talking to each other in the first place.

Maeterlinck wrote the story because he believed that the key to understanding ESP lay with animals. As well as being a writer, he was also a scientist who was interested in lots of different religions and spiritual paths, and many of his books are about what we now call the paranormal but was then called the occult. (Nowadays, "occult" is generally taken to mean superstitious stuff, because the meaning of words often changes over the years.)

As part of his researches, Maurice studied children who were mathematical prodigies. He found that they had a lower level of conscious intelligence in every other way — in other words, they were a bit dim at everything else — yet this seemed to allow their mathematical abilities to shine through from their subconscious.

He also studied Van Osten's horses and then conducted

other experiments with animals. Like the children who were brilliant at math, the animals had a lower conscious intelligence – they couldn't speak, or understand speech, and they couldn't do such things as placing different shaped pegs into the correct holes, as people could – but they scored highly in ESP tests.

As did people who were good at dowsing. And, guess what – these people didn't do very well at the intelligence tests.

Yet the funny thing was that the dowsers seemed to be very bad at the ESP tests at first – until Maurice looked at the results afterwards, and discovered that there was a pattern. It seemed that the dowsers couldn't tell him which card he was holding up – but they were telling him what he would hold up in three cards' time!

So precognition is part of ESP. Funny I should say that, as it seems that animals are very good at that particular form of ESP – as we'll soon discover.

QUESTIONS

◆◆ If Maeterlinck was right about people with lesser intelligence having more ESP, does this mean you can't be clever and have ESP?

◆◆ Do you think that Maeterlinck meant instead that the conscious mind – developed by learning and education – can sometimes get in the way of the unconscious mind? Have you ever experienced this?

Rupert Sheldrake and Testing Your Pet's ESP

Rupert Sheldrake is a scientist who for many years has been working on a theory that is connected to ESP. He believes that we are surrounded by energy fields that he calls biomorphic, and that we leave behind us "biomorphic resonance." This is a sort of shadow, and he believes that if you cut a shoot from a plant, a new one will grow in exactly the same place because it follows that shadow.

With humans, this works slightly differently. If you go out and leave your pet, you leave a part of your energy field behind. This grows weaker the further away you are, but becomes stronger the nearer you get to home. Rupert has noticed that some animals know when their owners are coming home, and suspects that this is because the animals are able to sense the biomorphic field growing stronger.

Perhaps this is so: it's certainly worth trying, so here's how ...

Is Your Pet Psychic?

You will need your pet and a friend to help you carry out this experiment.

First of all, you need to tell your friend how long you'll be out, and when you expect to be home. Then you go off somewhere, do something interesting, and remember to come home at the time you told your friend. Don't phone, because the pet may hear your voice on the phone, or associate the phone with your return home from other times, and therefore ruin the experiment.

When you get home, see if your friend noticed whether or not your pet acted strangely, as if knowing you were on your way. For instance, did the pet go to the front or back door, waiting for you? Did it suddenly wake up from a sleep just before you came in?

Then you repeat this experiment, always going out at different times, and varying the length of time you're out of the house. Make a table of the results. If the animal always seems to act oddly when you're on the way home, then you have a psychic pet!

And Another Thing ...

There's another experiment you might like to try, which is mentally to call your pet when you're in another room, or to see if the pet knows what you're thinking.

ESP With Animals • 65

For this, you should go into a separate room, then clear your mind and think about your pet coming to you. Think it in pictures, not words, as animals don't have language, and they think (scientists believe, and it seems reasonable) in pictures.

Does your pet come to you? How often?

Hide a ball, or your pet's favorite toy. Think about where it is and imagine your pet going to find it. See if it does, and how often.

Then think about your pet being fed. Think about putting food down for your pet, and see if it responds by going into the kitchen ...

Of course, the problem with this test is that any animal will dash to its food bowl at ANY time, given half a chance!

Anton Mesmer and Hypnotism

Hypnotism isn't an ESP power as such, but it does seem to be a gateway into the parts of the brain that give you ESP.

It's been around for as long as humanity – ancient priests used it to put people into trances – but the sort of hypnotism that we know now, and see on TV shows, is all due to Anton Franz Mesmer, a nineteenth-century Austrian doctor and experimenter who realized that subjects put into a trance using deep relaxation methods could be made to do whatever the hypnotist (or Mesmerist, as they were called after he wrote a book on the subject) wanted. People in hypnotic trances can do more than just act like idiots for the cameras. They can lose warts by the power of suggestion, be speared with needles and feel no pain, and if told they have been touched by a red-hot poker will develop burn marks and blisters.

What this shows is the power that the mind can have over the human body. It's as though this trance state enables the right-hand part of the brain to release a little more of its power by by-passing the left-hand part, which is out cold and doesn't have time to block ESP or other powers by worrying about whether you've done your homework or what to have for dinner.

A lot of the early experiments were carried out on animals, and were used in attempts to train them. It's incredibly easy to hypnotize a chicken – you draw a straight line and make the chicken focus its eyes on the line by putting its head on the mark. The chicken then goes into a trance!

But please don't try this with any chickens you may have flapping around. I'm not sure that they really like it. I know I wouldn't if someone put my head on a line on the ground and made me look at it!

Hypnotism is interesting in relation to ESP because a lot of people with ESP powers have to go into a trance before their powers start to work. In effect, they hypnotize themselves.

One of the strange side-effects of these experiments was that people who were hypnotized to remember things from their past started to remember past lives – they became other people from other times. Some people think this is proof of reincarnation – that we live many lives and when we die we are reborn as babies with a new identity. Maybe this is so, but if time is static, and we are the ones moving through it, as H.F. Saltmarsh believed, then it's more likely that persons under hypnosis are using their unleashed ESP to make contact with other people in other times. I suppose you could call that a form of time-travel.

People who have been hypnotized have also been able to do psychometry and practice remote viewing, so it could be suggested that hypnosis will unleash ESP powers.

Having said that, hypnosis is dangerous when practiced by people who haven't learned it properly, because even the best hypnotist doesn't actually know WHY it works. So if you want to practice self-hypnosis as a way of tapping any ESP potential you may have, it would be a good idea to learn all about it first from someone who is a qualified practitioner. And that could be rather expensive.

So make sure your mum and dad are sitting down before you ask them!

CHAPTER 5

Automatic Writing and Ghosts

Automatic writing is a very strange phenomenon. Those people who practice it and find that something is coming through from a place other than their own minds can often be open to ridicule. No matter what the results of their writings, there will always be some people who call them liars.

The Story of the Hidden Chapels

Something similar to this happened to two Englishmen called Frederick Bligh-Bond and John Alleyne, despite the fact that their researches uncovered two old chapels in the grounds of Glastonbury Abbey that had been hidden for hundreds of years.

In the early 1900s, both men were members of the Somerset Archeological Society. Their imagination was captured by the beautiful ruins of the old abbey at Glastonbury, and their favorite dream was that they would one day find something momentous that would add to people's knowledge of the abbey and how it used to look.

They did – but the way in which they did it gave them nothing but trouble.

John and Frederick were also interested in the paranormal – around this time there was an immense amount of research into spirits, ghosts, and all the things that are linked to ESP. This was partly because the airplane and the car had just been invented, and people were convinced that science was on the verge of a great breakthrough into the unknown. But part of it was also because fashionable men and women like Sir Arthur Conan Doyle – the man who wrote all the Sherlock Holmes stories – were interested, and their names made sure that stories about the paranormal got into the newspapers. And as TV and radio were still many years away, the newspapers were incredibly powerful.

Although Glastonbury is still quiet compared to the big cities, it's hard to imagine how sleepy and far away it must have seemed in those days. Life moved at a slower pace, and for young men like John and Frederick there was plenty of time to experiment.

John Alleyne found that he had a faculty for automatic writing. At first, little seemed to happen, but after a short while he found that he was writing a vast amount of words that seemed to come from nowhere. They didn't make that much sense at first, and it was only when he and Frederick examined them carefully that they realized they were in two old languages. One was Latin, the language of the Romans, and was of a sort known as monastic Latin because it was used by the monks in the manuscripts they wrote and illustrated. The second language was Old English. It might seem surprising that they wouldn't recognize English, but if you've ever seen Old English on parchments or manuscripts in a museum, you'll realize right away that English has changed so much over the centuries that the original is almost unrecognizable today.

Both John and Frederick were immensely excited by their discoveries. Neither of them thought that they had been contacted by a dead spirit. Instead, they thought that somehow John had succeeded in switching off his everyday, conscious mind, and had by-passed normal thinking to tap into something else.

Frederick later wrote a book about their experiences, in which he explained his ideas about what had happened. He believed that there is a collective mind, a pool of energy where all thoughts and ideas are gathered together. Because he and John were particularly interested in Glastonbury Abbey, they had managed to contact the collective mind and grasp ideas about the place.

Because that's what appeared to be happening. Both Frederick and John were well-educated, and in those days that meant that they had studied old languages. As a result, they were able to translate what John had written while in his trance-like state.

The writings appeared to be from three monks – Brother Johannes, Abbot Beere, and Brother Ambrosius – who claimed to have lived in the abbey several centuries before. The writings were very straightforward, and described two chapels that lay in the grounds of the abbey. They gave directions saying where the chapels were located, measurements that showed how big they were, and even a couple of simple sketches to show how they were designed and laid out in the grounds.

Both John and Frederick were immensely excited: this was their chance to do something wonderful for the abbey, as they had always wished. They approached the Church authorities at Glastonbury for permission to start excavating at the site. As they were rather worried about people believing their story, they kept quiet about how they got the information. Fortunately, Frederick Bligh-Bond was by now a qualified architect, so the Church authorities assumed that he had obtained the information by research into old documents – which, in a way, he had!

The work at the abbey grounds took some time. As both men were still members of the Somerset Archeological Society, obtaining volunteers wasn't hard. But the foundations would be buried some way down, and work had to be very slow and careful in order not to destroy any fragile remains.

The first chapel – the Edgar Chapel – was uncovered in 1908. It was exactly where the monks (or whatever had appeared as the monks' writing) had told John it would be. Every detail was correct.

It was another 11 years before the Loretto Chapel was unearthed, in 1919. Work had been slow, and had been interrupted by World War I, but when the chapel was revealed it was again exactly where the automatic writings had described it.

The Church authorities were delighted with what had been found, and John and Frederick were hailed as heroes. Which they probably would have remained if they had maintained their silence about where the information had come from. But they were honest men, and were as excited by the manner in which they had obtained their information as by what they had found at the site. Before the first excavation had even begun, they had left their manuscripts in a sealed envelope with Sir William Barrett, a respected professor at Dublin University and a well-known figure in the Society for Psychical Research. He swore that he would not open the envelope until the excavations were complete.

When he did, he was astounded. He wanted to publish the manuscripts, but John and Frederick asked him to stay silent until they had finished their own book on the story. He was happy to do this, and agreed to write a foreword.

The book – credited to Frederick Bligh-Bond, who wrote their story, while John supplied his automatic writings and drawings – was called *The Gate of Remembrance*, and was published to a reaction that was the last thing that both men had expected.

The Church authorities accused both men of being fakes and cheats, and tried to stop the book being published. When it emerged in the shops, they tried to buy up every copy. In Somerset, the men found that all their friends and their families' friends had turned against them.

They couldn't understand what was wrong: they had found two beautiful old ruins that would otherwise have been lost, and they had obtained their information in a way that showed some remarkable abilities of the human mind. Surely people would want to know about this? Apparently not: perhaps people were more scared of the unknown than they had thought.

The stress and pressure of being treated in this way made John Alleyne ill, and he died at a young age. Frederick Bligh-Bond emigrated to America, where he made a career as an architect. He never returned to Somerset. The book vanished from the shelves for over 50 years until it was republished in the late 1970s, recognized at last as a remarkable work of research into the faculty of ESP. What couldn't be hidden were the chapels, which are still to be seen in the grounds of Glastonbury Abbey.

Although what happened to John and Frederick was terrible, having the ability to write automatically and be open and honest about it isn't always a cause for trouble.

The Old Woman Who Could Write in Russian

Michael Bentine, the late comedian, actor and writer, was possibly the only full-blooded Peruvian who could claim to be born in Watford, north of London. Apart from his brother, that is.

Not that Michael was the old woman who could write in Russian. Although he created many comic characters and puppets in his time, an old woman writing in Russian wasn't one of them! He did have a lot of interesting stories to tell about such people, though.

Michael had a facility for ESP all his life, even when he didn't know what it was. When he was very young, his family moved to Hastings, on the south coast of England. The area had been heavily occupied during Roman times, and young Michael would lie on the hillside watching Roman legions tramp through the valleys. He thought for a long time that it was merely his vivid imagination – but maybe it wasn't. (Skip ahead two chapters if you can't wait to find out more!)

In the 1930s, when he was a boy, Michael and his brother used to follow their dad as he trekked around Kent investigating psychic phenomena. Dad was a scientist and inventor who had become interested in the idea that the so-called "supernatural" would be easily explained once someone found a way to do so. So he thought it might be a good idea to look into the supernatural: as he had worked with lots of famous physicists on what would eventually become nuclear power, he knew virtually everything there was to know about how far science had come.

On one visit, Michael met a remarkable woman. She was hidden away in a little Kentish village, and was very matter-of-fact about her way of recording automatic writing. While Michael watched in amazement, she chatted to a stream of visitors about local gossip, paying no attention to what she was writing down. Unlike some automatic writers, she had no need to go into a trance or to sit in a quiet room so that she could "switch off" her conscious mind. Instead, she seemed to distract it with her visitors and the goings-on of her friends and neighbors. And all the while she scribbled away, her hands flying over the paper.

Hands?

Yes. Even more bizarre, she was writing with both hands at the same time. But more on that later. For now, what's really amazing is what she was writing.

Having been astounded by the fact that she could write

with both hands, Michael had expected that when his dad examined the sheets of paper, they would have nothing but gibberish on them. And so it looked to him – but not to his dad.

While she had been merrily gossiping away, and without seeming even to look at what she was doing, the old woman had written several sheets of Russian script, academic French, technically exact German, and advanced mathematics as well as very precise English.

Now this truly was astounding, because the old woman confessed that normally she found it hard to put pen to paper and write a letter. Her everyday written English was nowhere near as precise as that she produced when writing automatically, which was more like a professor's academic essay.

As for Russian, German and French – she knew none of them, and admitted she wouldn't know which one was which if it was put in front of her. In fact, she had no idea what she had been writing.

And as for the mathematics – well, she admitted that she had trouble adding up her shopping at the grocer's. Sums were not her strong point. Yet she was writing things that Michael's dad had trouble following!

When she was asked if she knew where her writing came from, she told them that she neither knew nor cared. It was simply something that she had an urge to do every now and then. She didn't think about it – just let it happen until it went away for a while.

Michael's dad took away the sheets of paper and had the writing analyzed by language experts. He could speak several languages and had recognized them at once, just as he had recognized the math as being genuine. But he wanted to know to what level they were exact. Was it the sort of German you would learn to go on holiday, or was it the sort of Russian or French you would only find inside a university library? They were the latter: this was the sort of writing that could only be done by a scholar in each language.

So what was the answer? A skeptic would say that the woman knew all these languages and only pretended to be ordinary. But why? If she was doing this on the stage or radio, it would have made sense to act like this. But she lived quietly in a small village, and wasn't very well off.

The only answer could be that she had a gift of ESP but wasn't even aware of what it was!

QUESTIONS

- Is it possible that Frederick and John, or the old woman who could write Russian, knew about these topics before they started automatic writing?

- If they had learned these things, and had forgotten that they had come across them, then is it possible that their unconscious minds recalled them and pushed them out through automatic writing?

- But if you think this is possible, then how do you explain the fact that the old woman had virtually no education yet was writing to university standard? And how would Frederick and John have found out about a part of the abbey that had been lost for centuries?

Writing Two Things at the Same Time

What had really made Michael's jaw drop at first was seeing the old woman write with both hands at the same time. A lot of people can do this without having the remotest hint of any ESP. Especially people who were born left-handed.

I was born left-handed – I still throw a cricket or tennis ball with my left hand – yet I was made right-handed. When I first started school, it was my natural inclination to write with my left hand but my teacher didn't approve of this and I was forced to write with my right. As a result, my handwriting has always been pretty bad. I also learned most other things right-handed (I play the guitar this way – and pretty badly. If I'd started out left-handed, I might even have been a rock star!), but always threw left-handed for some reason. Oddly enough, I can't write left-handed.

But I have a friend who is left-handed, and her teachers never made her write with her right hand. As a result, she's able to write with both hands, which is called being ambidextrous (from the Latin, meaning "with both hands"). She doesn't have any ESP.

So what, you may well be wondering, has being left-handed got to do with ESP? Well, nothing directly, except this: the brain works in two halves, as we saw earlier. The left-hand side of the brain controls the right-hand side of the body, and vice versa. Most right-handed people, therefore, control their writing hand from the left side of their brain. But this means that left-handed people have their writing hands controlled by the opposite side of their brain to that used by everyone else.

So does this mean that the brain is able to switch around what it can do? To a certain extent, yes. And if you're writing with a part of the brain that doesn't usually control writing – that's to say, you're right-handed but you try writing with your left – then who knows what you're making your brain do!

So, if you really want to try automatic writing and all you've ever come up with is a few scribbles about your daydreams (I know that's all I ever write down when I try!), then try switching hands and see what you can do. And if you're really excited by the idea, try it with both hands.

The brain is a complex organ that no one really understands. As I've already explained, we only use a small part of it. Maybe it has the ability to tap into all these ideas that are out there in the information universe, and ESP is the facility that makes us able to do that. And maybe all you need is a little trick like this to bypass your conscious mind.

Remember: don't be scared by anything that comes out on paper, especially if you have no idea what you have been writing. ESP never hurt or harmed anyone. What can harm you is being frightened of something that is happening naturally. If you do become scared, stop writing.

There are very few people with the level of ESP that means these abilities are always with them. And they are usually ready for it and welcome it (as we'll see in the next section). If you don't want it, ESP will go away.

Automatic Writing

This is really easy to do. Just take a sheet of paper and sit down with (if you really want to go for it) a pen in each hand. Try to think of nothing – don't even look at the paper. And just let the pens go over the paper.

See what you've got when you've filled up each sheet. Does any of it make sense? Do you remember thinking any of it while you were writing?

If there are words or phrases on the paper that make sense and which you don't recall writing, then maybe something has come through from your subconscious.

See if anything that you've written comes true in any way. If you've written something that refers to someone you know, or a place or time that you can check out, see how accurate your forecast was.

Are There Really Such Things as Ghosts?

Yes. I mean, no. No – yes. I mean yes, there are no – oh look, let's start again.

It's not a question that can be answered simply. Why? Because, in order for a question to be answered, you have to know what it means. And what IS a ghost, anyway?

Really, the best thing to do is to start like this. Some people see figures that aren't really there: people, animals, even buses or buildings. Honest! In the 1960s a ghostly bus in London caused several accidents in one road, because drivers would swerve to avoid it and then find it wasn't there any more! So, if you call that a ghost, then they do exist. Not everyone can see them – I wouldn't see a ghost if it came up and hit me over the head – but I know several people who can see or hear things that I can't.

But what are these ghosts? Some people say that ghosts are the spirits of the dead that haven't moved beyond the physical plane to the next plane of existence. This is heaven if you're a Christian, nirvana if you're a Buddhist, and so on. There is definitely a certain amount of evidence to suggest this. In 1977, a house in Enfield, North London, was being haunted by a poltergeist. Some people believe that poltergeists are bursts of ESP energy that come from young people who don't know what's happening to them. But some believe that poltergeists are what are called discarnate spirits – spirits that have intelligence but no body. A medium called Domo Gmelig-Meyer came over from Holland and held a seance in the Enfield house. A remarkable cassette recording taken at the time has several people talking in different voices to the medium.

They all gave their names and were quite annoyed when they were told that they had died. They didn't seem to realize what had happened. Guy Lyon Playfair, a researcher who was at the seance, was interested to know if there was any truth in these claims. He found that one of the named voices was an old man who had lived in the haunted house, and that others who were named were buried near the old man in the local cemetery.

Playfair liked to keep an open mind about this, and I agree with him. When I studied physics at school, one of the first things we learned was that energy does not disappear or dissipate. It cannot be destroyed but turns into something else. What powers us is electricity – energy. When we die, that spark of life has to go somewhere. Which, I suppose, is rather like the idea of souls going to heaven or nirvana. But – and this is what people have been arguing about for centuries – does that spark of energy retain our memories and personality: the things that make me me, and you you?

I'm not sure. Neither was Playfair in this instance, and

although he would never accuse Gmelig-Meyer of lying, he says that it is also possible that he was picking up memories and thoughts that were simply "lying around." Which is equally likely – and just goes to show why it's so difficult to pin down what ESP in its many forms lets us see.

Then again, there are some ghosts that do the same thing over and over again. There are two good examples of this. One is at the famous Borley Rectory, which was once Britain's most haunted house. Although the Rectory was burnt down during World War II, the ghost of a nun that haunted the grounds still walks there.

In fact, that's all she does. She walks up one side of the garden and down the other in a straight line, as though she were following a path. In a similar way, there is a ghost in Bradley Woods, just outside Grimsby, in northern England. Dressed in black, with a shining white face, she always walks the same route through the woods and across a field that was once part of the woods. Several people have seen her, including a motorcyclist who crashed his bike trying to

avoid running her down! Robin Furman, the psychologist and paranormal investigator, studied this case for the local paper, the *Grimsby Evening Telegraph*, after he was approached by a couple who had seen the woman. His appeal for other sightings led to a number of reports and stories, and he eventually found an old man living a few miles away, in Cleethorpes, who thought he might know who the woman was.

During World War I, Bradley Woods had been used as an army training camp, and some of the soldiers staying in the woods found a woman who was about to have a baby. She was obviously living rough in the woods, and was in agony. The baby was born dead and the soldiers loaded the young woman into a wheelbarrow – the best they could find at such short notice – and took her to the nearest doctor. The old man in Cleethorpes was a young boy at the time, and would sell food to the soldiers when their instructors weren't around. He and his friend helped the soldiers.

Sadly, the young woman was dead by the time they reached the doctor, despite their best efforts. The route they had taken was the same as that walked by the ghostly figure.

Robin's idea is that the ghost is a revenant (which comes from a French word meaning "something that keeps returning") – a part of the woman's life energy that keeps replaying like a video tape, again and again, looking for her baby.

The theory that ghosts are like tape recordings is an interesting one. Tom Lethbridge was a great believer in this idea, and noticed that the ghost he kept seeing when he first moved to Cornwall always appeared in the same spot, doing the same thing, near a stream. He had an idea that the magnetic energy that occurs near water acted as some kind of tape recorder.

There is no single, clear theory about this, but there is general agreement about how the tape recordings work. Something happens on a site that involves a lot of emotions or energy – it could be someone dying, like the young woman, or it could be a marching army, like the Romans that Michael Bentine saw as a boy – and the magnetic energy in the earth and water acts like a video tape to record all this. People who have some kind of ESP faculty are able to "switch on" the tape without realizing it, and therefore can see what happened years before.

That might sound peculiar, but perhaps it isn't when you remember that cassettes work on a magnetic principle. You can even make a simple metal recorder yourself with a strip of wire which you have magnetized and a pile of rusty metal filings. The magnetic wire will attract the filings in a pattern that can reproduce whatever sound you wish to record. The rust acts like the oxide that you see mentioned on cassette cases. So maybe some places are able to record something on to the magnetics that are in the earth?

Right – so ghosts are either dead people (or parts of them) that haven't gone away, or are tape recordings from the past. Anything else?

Oh yes – the idea that they aren't "ghosts" so much as real objects that have broken through time in some way. Remember how H.T. Saltmarsh had the idea that time was static, and that we moved through it only seeing what was directly ahead of us? In effect, he said that time doesn't move, we do, and this prevents us seeing that absolutely everything is happening around us all at once. Well, some researchers have put forward the idea that ghosts are things breaking through from other times – or, indeed, that people with ESP are the ones breaking through into another time!

Since that last sentence has confused me a bit, let's look at a story that makes it clearer. Matthew Manning is one of the most famous people with ESP powers alive today. From a very young age, strange things happened around him. He saw ghosts and heard voices, and strange writings and drawings would appear on the walls of his house while he was out, or in another room. One of the oddest things that happened was that he saw a ghost – the ghost of someone who was dressed like an Elizabethan.

Matthew would talk to this ghost – and you'd expect him to ask the ghost what on earth it was doing in his house. But no! It was the ghost who got quite annoyed with Matthew, and who told him off for appearing in HIS house! To the Elizabethan man, who was going about his everyday business, it was Matthew who was the strange apparition appearing in his home.

And it can happen without you even realizing it. In 1901, two schoolteachers were on holiday in Paris and visited the gardens at the Palace of Versailles. Once, this was the home of the French royal family.

The two teachers were walking in the gardens when they noticed a number of people dressed as they would have been over 100 years before. They spoke to one of them, and admired the gardens. It was only later, when they looked at their guidebook, that they realized the gardens in the book were laid out in a totally different fashion from those they had admired. And when they asked a guide about the fancy-dress party they had seen earlier, he was puzzled. They took him to where they had seen the people, and were astonished to find the gardens laid out completely differently from those they had sat in. It seemed that they had jumped back in time. So who were the ghosts – the people they had seen, or they themselves?

Are ghosts any of these things, or all of them? Until it can be positively proved, and experiments can repeat some remarkable results that have only appeared once or twice, we won't be able to say for certain.

One thing is definite: people who have ESP seem able to dip into these things that are happening around us and that we can't always see. Someone with ESP once said that if we could see everything that was happening all around us with crystal clarity, we'd never do anything because it would too much for us to take in at once, and we would never be able to sort out which bits of it we needed in order to go about our daily business.

So perhaps ESP is a way in which some remarkable people can see some more elements of this world: their brains and minds don't filter out a lot of the information they receive, but allow them a glimpse into things that the rest of us can only guess at.

CHAPTER 6

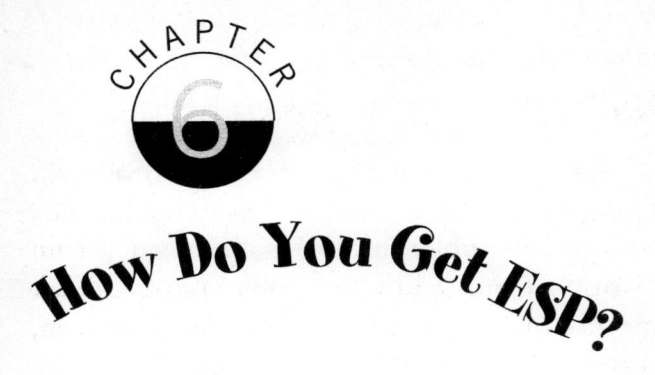

How Do You Get ESP?

Although I've just said that people with ESP are remarkable and few and far between, this isn't necessarily the case. Perhaps it would be better to say that those people who know they have these faculties, and who have developed them in some way, are few and far between. For, while there are some people who seem to be incapable of ESP for some reason (in the same way that I can't ride a bike because I have an inner ear problem that affects my balance), most people have the ability to develop some small degree of ESP. It takes time, practice, and the ability to spot which kind of ESP you have a knack for – but it can be done.

But Does It Happen by Accident?

Whether or not this is always intentional is another matter. A perfect example of this is Peter Hurkos, a Dutch psychic who became world-famous in the 1950s and 1960s after he was taken to America by a rich businessman whose son was missing. This businessman wanted Hurkos to find the boy, and had asked scientist and psychic researcher Andrija Puharich to find a genuine psychic. Puharich knew about Hurkos, and flew him over to the States.

Hurkos found the boy – but too late, for he had already drowned in a boating accident, which was why he was missing. The amount of publicity Hurkos received led to other offers of work – from the police among others – and he stayed in America.

But Peter Hurkos hadn't always been a psychic. In fact, he had originally been a housepainter with absolutely no ESP powers at all. During the first 30 years of his life he grew up and became an ordinary housepainter in Holland.

This changed for ever on July 10, 1941. Pieter Van Der Hurk (his real name) was up a ladder when he slipped and fell. He broke his shoulder, but more importantly he hit his head and suffered concussion. He was blind for three days and could remember nothing of the fall, only that he had seen his life flash before his eyes.

Pieter's wife came to visit him in hospital, and often their son would come with her. But one day she had left him with their neighbor when Pieter suddenly became alarmed and started shouting at her to rush home because their neighbor's house was on fire. She did – only to find that everything was all right. A few days later, the neighbor's house burnt to the ground.

Pieter couldn't explain why he had suddenly said that the

house was on fire, but did say that a picture of it had come into his mind. He also couldn't explain why he suddenly told his nurse one morning to be careful on a train because she might lose a suitcase. She gave him a funny look and said that she had lost a suitcase on the train coming to work that very morning – and how did he know?

Then one morning he turned to the patient in the next bed and told him how wicked he was to have sold the watch his father gave him – the watch that his father had worked so hard to buy for him. The young man in the next bed agreed that he was ashamed to have sold it – but then asked Pieter how he knew about this, since the young man had only been admitted to hospital that morning, and hadn't yet spoken to Pieter.

Gradually, it began to dawn on Pieter that something had happened to him when he fell off the ladder. Somehow, he had been given a glimpse into other people's minds.

It was a talent that nearly got him killed, because this was during World War II and Holland was occupied by the Nazis. The Dutch resistance movement heard about Pieter and were suspicious of how he came by his knowledge: the patient who had sold his watch was also a member of the resistance, and had reported back about the man who knew too much. The resistance decided that Pieter must be a Nazi spy to be so well informed – and that he must be killed to prevent resistance members being betrayed.

One night, two members of the resistance sneaked into the hospital and attacked Pieter in his bed. One of them began to smother Pieter with a pillow, but stopped suddenly because Pieter had yelled out the name of the man's mother, and asked how she was. How did he know her name, and that she had been ill? Especially as the man was sure that Pieter hadn't seen his face, and wouldn't know who he was.

Pieter was taken away by the resistance, and after close

questioning became a member of the resistance instead of a target! His talents were used to determine whether potential new recruits were genuine or Nazi spies. As all resistance members adopted new names for security purposes, he became Peter Hurkos – the name he kept after the war when he took his talents on to the stage with a mind-reading act.

The fact that it took a blow on the head for Peter Hurkos to suddenly develop ESP talent is interesting: after all, if the brain is the key to who does or doesn't have ESP powers, then it could be possible that a blow on the head somehow causes a "short-circuit" in the brain that links parts that otherwise don't connect with your conscious mind.

But this doesn't mean you should go around hitting yourself on the head to try to develop ESP!

Something similar happened to Peter Fairley, who was the science correspondent for the British TV news company ITN. In 1965, Peter had a brain virus that left him temporarily blind. When he recovered, he found that he had "second sight." This is a very mild form of ESP that meant he was able to pick winners from a horserace because the name of the winner would seem to leap up at him from the page. He also thought about doing some charity work for blind people literally seconds before the phone rang and he was asked if he would help. He made a TV program about his experiences and the way that they seemed to tail off the longer time went on, until eventually they disappeared.

What's interesting about this is the way in which the ESP, when it appears, seems to become like the personality of the person involved. Peter Hurkos was a very flamboyant man, and he had big visions that made him famous and helped him to solve crimes. But Peter Fairley was a very down-to-earth man, and his experiences of ESP were very minor, mundane things.

This is very similar to the way in which two women called Suzanne Padfield and Estelle Roberts viewed their own ESP powers. Both women had accidents at home that seemed to spark off their ESP, yet both viewed them totally differently, as we'll discover in a minute.

QUESTIONS

◆▸ Is there any way, other than ESP, that Pieter could have known those details about the resistance man who tried to kill him?

◆▸ Similarly, is it possible that he could have overheard someone talking about the watch or the suitcase?

◆▸ If this is so, is there any way he could have found out about the house being burned down – even if it was a week away. Or could this have been coincidence?

Estelle and Suzanne

Estelle Roberts was born at the end of the nineteenth century and was an extremely famous psychic in the years between the two world wars. During the 1920s and 1930s she held regular talks at the Conway Hall, in central London, that sold out and had people lining up around the block. She would relay messages that she believed came from the spirit world, but which could just as easily have been mind-reading.

Suzanne Padfield lives quietly away from the limelight. During the 1970s she worked with the researcher Benson Herbert – who had ESP powers himself – at his laboratory in Hampshire. She married a scientist, and firmly believes that her powers come from her brain and not from the world of spirits.

Yet both women had very similar experiences when they were children. Suzanne would see a ghost which came up to her bed and touched her. This was followed by a series of brilliant lights that would appear in her bedroom. Then there were the strange poltergeist happenings.

As you may remember, poltergeists were mentioned briefly in the previous chapter: some people believe that poltergeists are bursts of directionless energy given off by people with ESP powers (usually girls, but no one knows why). Others believe that they are ghosts that aren't visible in any way. What usually happens with poltergeists is that things get flung about the room, objects disappear and reappear in strange places, and chaos ensues.

This is what happened to Suzanne for a short while. In fact, on one occasion a clothes horse full of washing disappeared from her parents' kitchen and was never seen again! The ghosts and strange lights persisted, and it was only when she had grown up that Suzanne decided that these things came from inside her mind, and not from spirits that were outside.

Estelle, on the other hand, felt differently. Her experiences started when she was a small girl, just like Suzanne, and one of the first things that happened to her was when a knight in shining armour appeared at her bedroom window (which was two floors up) one night, tapping on the window pane. Estelle and her sister were both in the bedroom, and both saw the knight. Estelle was fascinated and wanted to invite the knight into the room. But her sister was frightened, and turned her head away.

Now here's something very important to remember if you find ESP and everything connected with it slightly frightening. Estelle was a medium all her life, and she wanted the knight to come in: her sister, who turned away and didn't want to know, never had another psychic experience in her life. Which just goes to show that if you don't want these things to happen to you, they won't.

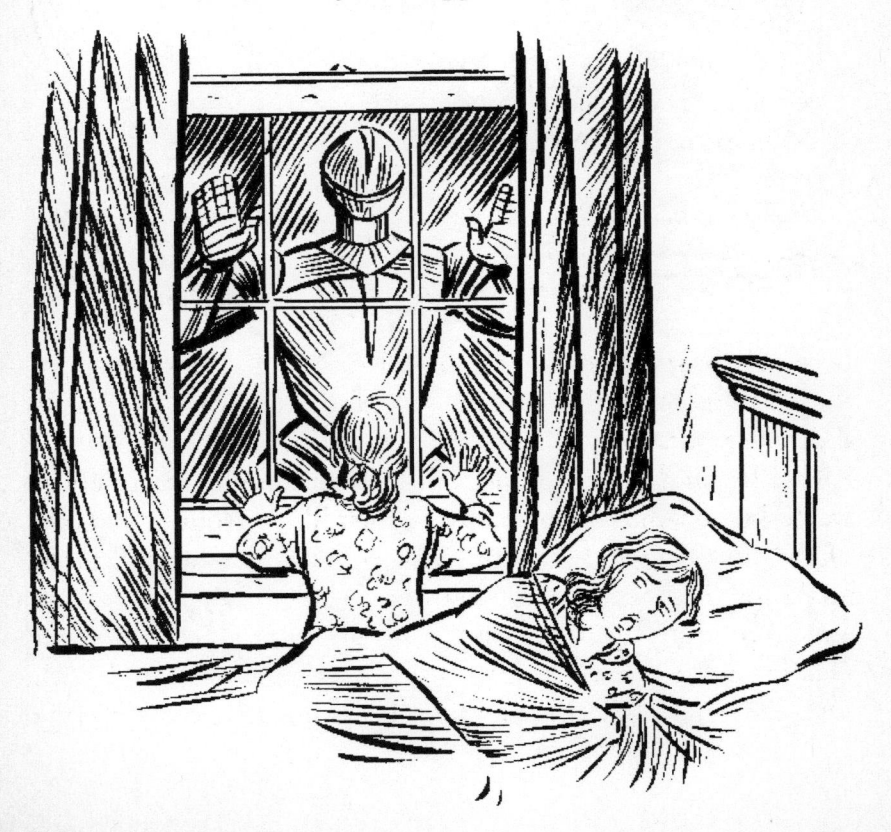

But for Estelle, these psychic phenomena kept being repeated. She found herself being flung out of bed in the middle of the night. Once, this happened several times in quick succession, and at one point her father found her floating over the stairs. At the same time, a fire started in the downstairs drawing room.

Suzanne, at a similar age, often found herself flung out of bed. Later, when she was working at Benson Herbert's laboratory, she was able to make a table levitate simply by touching it, in much the same way as Estelle had been able to levitate herself.

Yet Estelle was convinced that it was the work of spirits, and Suzanne grew up to believe that it was something new and eventually explainable that came from her own mind.

Why would these two women look at similar experiences in such contrasting ways? Part of the reason is the different times in which they lived. When Estelle was young, there was a great belief in Spiritualism, which still has its own church. Spiritualists, who are basically Christian, believe that the spirits of the dead can talk to us from heaven, and if you have the gift of ESP then you can communicate with them.

When Suzanne was at the peak of her powers, in the 1970s, science firmly believed that it was on the edge of a breakthrough, and that all ESP could be explained as the workings of parts of the brain that were only just beginning to be used by human beings. As a result, Suzanne felt that the ghost she had seen was a tape-recorded figure that was part of her parents' house, and that the poltergeist effects she had experienced were coming from her brain, and not from an outside spirit.

Even when both women were grown up, and their ESP was still active, they "saw" things differently. A good example of this is the way that they both reacted to the disappearance of missing children they were asked to help find.

In 1937, a young girl called Mona Tinsley had been missing for some time. When Estelle was asked to help, she saw the girl as a spirit that came to her and told her about the river where her body could be found. Sure enough, that's where she was.

In 1980, a Russian girl called Inessa Tchurina was missing. She, too, was dead and her body was in a river. But Suzanne helped to locate her by holding some of her clothing, and through psychometry was able to "see" what had happened to her as though she were watching a film in front of her closed eyes.

This is something interesting you find with people who have such ESP powers: what they believe the powers to be makes them "see" things in a certain way. Because Estelle believed in Spiritualism, she saw the information as coming from a ghost. And because Suzanne believed in the powers of her own brain, she saw the information in a totally different manner.

This really illustrates one of the reasons why ESP is so hard to pin down scientifically: it's almost as if the brain plays tricks on us, and lets people with ESP see things in whichever way they are most likely to find believable.

QUESTIONS

◆✦ Because Suzanne and Estelle both felt that their powers came from different sources – their brains or the spirits of the dead – then is it possible that both of them were wrong and their powers come from some source we don't yet know about?

◆✦ Alternatively, why shouldn't both ideas be true? Do you think that there is one BIG answer to ESP, or lots of little answers? If people see things in different ways, could it be because there are different reasons for them doing so?

The Amazing Story of Uri Geller

Uri was born in 1946 in an area of Palestine that is now the Israeli city of Tel Aviv. His parents were Jewish refugees from Hungary who had arrived after the end of World War II, and it wasn't long before the young Uri was taken by his mother to live in Cyprus. He didn't return to Israel until he was 18, when he came back to serve as a paratrooper in the Israeli Army. This was during the Six Day War of 1967, and Uri was injured. He was allowed to spend the rest of his national service acting as an instructor at a youth camp.

Ever since he was a child, Uri had known that he had strange powers, and had long been able to influence clocks and make cutlery bend when he touched it. He didn't know where this power came from, and he'd given it little thought.

While he was at the youth camp, he would do tricks to amuse himself and others, such as making the clocks speed up and bending the cutlery in the canteen.

One of the young people at the youth camp was a 14-year-old boy called Shipi Shtrang. He was fascinated by Uri, and asked him why he was an instructor at a youth camp instead of being on stage, earning lots of money with his act. Uri thought about it, and then replied that there was really no reason ... no reason at all.

So Uri Geller had found himself a manager in Shipi Shtrang – who even became his brother-in-law when Uri married Shipi's sister, Hannah. As Shipi was so young, Uri made his way on his own to begin with, but he didn't forget who had first suggested that he attempt to exploit his remarkable powers.

In less than a year, Uri had become a star in Israel. He appeared on TV bending metal and making broken watches start. Newspapers wrote about him, and he was even used as a male model. In fact, he became so famous that when a reporter asked the Prime Minister, Golda Meir, what the future of Israel would be, she replied that perhaps he should ask Uri!

By 1970, the Magic Circle of Israel (the professional body of magicians) were going all-out to prove that Uri was doing everything by magic and illusion, and that his powers weren't real. Things were getting a bit hot, especially as Uri's powers were beginning to fail him on TV now and again.

He didn't know why his powers would stop and start, but Uri was under a lot of pressure: every time a TV program booked him, they would expect him to start a watch or bend a spoon. But it didn't happen every time: Uri found that the more pressure people put on him, the more difficult it was for him to achieve a result. Thinking about it, he was sure this was because the stress of having to perform well was preventing whatever part of his mind did these things from working.

With all this pressure, Uri was glad when a physicist called Dr Andrija Puharich arrived in Israel, saying that he had funds to take Uri to the USA and conduct a series of studies on his powers. Arriving at the Stanford Research Institute in California, he underwent two series of rigorous tests. These involved his abilities to start watches and bend metal, and also explored his ability to predict what would happen with a series of cards, and to discover if he was able to use psychometry and "see" events from holding objects.

Puharich examined the results of the tests – conducted in conditions that were totally different from those of TV shows, and in which Uri (or anyone else) wouldn't have been able to cheat – and announced that he was genuine.

Shipi arranged tours of the USA, with appearances on such nationwide TV programs as Johnny Carson's *Tonight* show – which had the largest number of viewers of any program in the world at that time – and live shows where Uri would show off his talents. Once again, Uri was being overworked, and sometimes there would be no result when he tried to use his powers. It was very difficult, because there were people waiting for him to fail. For instance, a professional magician called James Randi was convinced that Uri was a fake, and has spent many years trying to disprove everything he has ever done. Eventually, Uri had to take Randi to court. Uri won.

After these tours, there were more tests: Eldon Byrd was a high-ranking naval officer and physicist who was investigating the new area of parascience for the US government, and he put Uri through a series of tests at Kent State University in Ohio, and the Naval Surface Weapons Center in Maryland. The result of these tests was the first report on parascience that was taken seriously by the US government.

Now the FBI wanted to use Uri! He found himself looking at maps, trying to locate the position of a kidnapped boy. He thought the boy was being held in a warehouse (although he couldn't say why he felt this), and he was able to suggest a few streets where the warehouse might be. The following night the FBI recovered the boy from a warehouse in the area that Uri had indicated. After this, he was whisked up in a helicopter to find a yacht that was being used by drug-runners.

All of this frightened Uri – what if the Mafia and similar gangs found out that he was helping the FBI and CIA to hunt them down? He was worried that they might try to kill him. And the more frightened he became, the more difficult it was to get results – once again, Uri's idea that the more stress he felt the more it interfered with his ESP seemed to be coming true.

By the end of the 1970s, Uri had had enough of showbusiness and being used as a psychic detective.

In 1973, Uri had been introduced to Sir Val Duncan, a British industrialist who told Uri he could make a lot of money from his talents, and then introduced Uri to the art of dowsing. As an experiment, Sir Val gave Uri a map of some territories owned by his company in South America. They were looking for mineral deposits but didn't have a survey of the land and were reluctant to start drilling operations blindly as it is so expensive. So Uri stood over the map with his pendulum and found a spot on the map to which the pendulum responded. Sir Val instructed his team to survey the spot, and they found the mineral deposits they had been looking for.

Gold, silver, minerals, you name it – with an adjustment to a pendulum, Uri found that he could locate all of these by standing in an office with just a series of maps. So he decided to hire himself out to interested companies – but he wouldn't charge a fee! Instead, he would ask for a fraction of one per cent on any money that was made from finds on the sites he selected.

Because he was so good, and because word spread about his results, Uri Geller became another sort of great success, and without having to bend any spoons.

QUESTIONS

◆✦ Do you think it was a mistake for Uri to appear on TV knowing that he wouldn't always get a result?

◆✦ Why do you think people expected him to be right all the time, even when he told them his powers didn't work that way?

◆✦ If you had been Uri, what would you have done? Would you have tried to explain why your powers didn't always work, or would you have tried to make yourself look good, knowing you were genuine?

Nella's Telly

Nella Jones is a British psychic who is best known for her work with the police on criminal cases. This started when she was brought in by the family of a kidnaped girl to help the police find where she was being held. Nella wasn't able to tell the police very much, but was rather bewildered to find herself delivering ransom money to a wastebin in a public park.

Since that time, a number of police officers have turned to Nella when they've felt that a psychic could help in some way – usually when the normal methods of detection have reached a dead end and there is a race against time to get something done.

This was one reason why Nella was once again asked to help when the real estate agent Stephanie Slater was kidnaped in 1990 by Michael Sams, a criminal on the run. Nella was able to give the police a description of the kidnaper and this tallied with the one Stephanie gave police when she was released. The information that she was able to give them about the make of Sams' car helped to capture him.

But by far the nastiest case Nella was involved in was one where her evidence was lost in a mass of paperwork. When it was found, it helped to piece together a little more information about the man the police had captured.

For several years in the late 1970s and very early 1980s, Yorkshire was terrorized by a killer the police called the Yorkshire Ripper – partly because he was as mysterious and hard to capture as Jack The Ripper, and partly because, like Jack, he only killed women. It was a frightening time to be a young woman in any Yorkshire town, and the police were frantic to catch him.

Yet the bizarre thing is that Nella had no direct involvement with the police on this case. At that time, she was still known mostly for her concert hall appearances: like Estelle Roberts in the 1920s and 1930s, and contemporary mediums like Doris Stokes and Doris Collins, Nella appeared in large halls where people would line up to come to hear her speak, hoping that she would be able to give them a message from a dead relative.

Nella had made enough of a name for herself for a publisher to offer her the chance to write her autobiography. Since she found this difficult to do on her own, a journalist called Shirley Davenport was hired by the publisher to assist Nella in getting her life story down on paper. One evening, just after Shirley had left Nella's house, the strangest thing happened. Nella switched on the television to watch the early evening news, and there was a report about the latest killing in Yorkshire. While Nella watched, it seemed to her as though there were two pictures appearing on the screen.

As well as that day's news report, it was as though she was seeing a news report from the future: it was after the killer had been captured, and the news report was about him. But because there were two things going on at once, the screen was fuzzy and the sound difficult to follow. It was as though two pieces of film had been superimposed on one another, making each one difficult to understand.

What Nella could pick out was this: the name of the killer was Peter, and he was a truck driver. He came from Bradford, and lived in a house on a hill with the number six. He drove a truck for a living, and part of the name on the door of the truck began with a "C". But the terrible thing about the vision was that the newscaster was talking about another killing that had taken place on November 17. It was the middle of October so Nella was frightened that, if she didn't act, another woman would die.

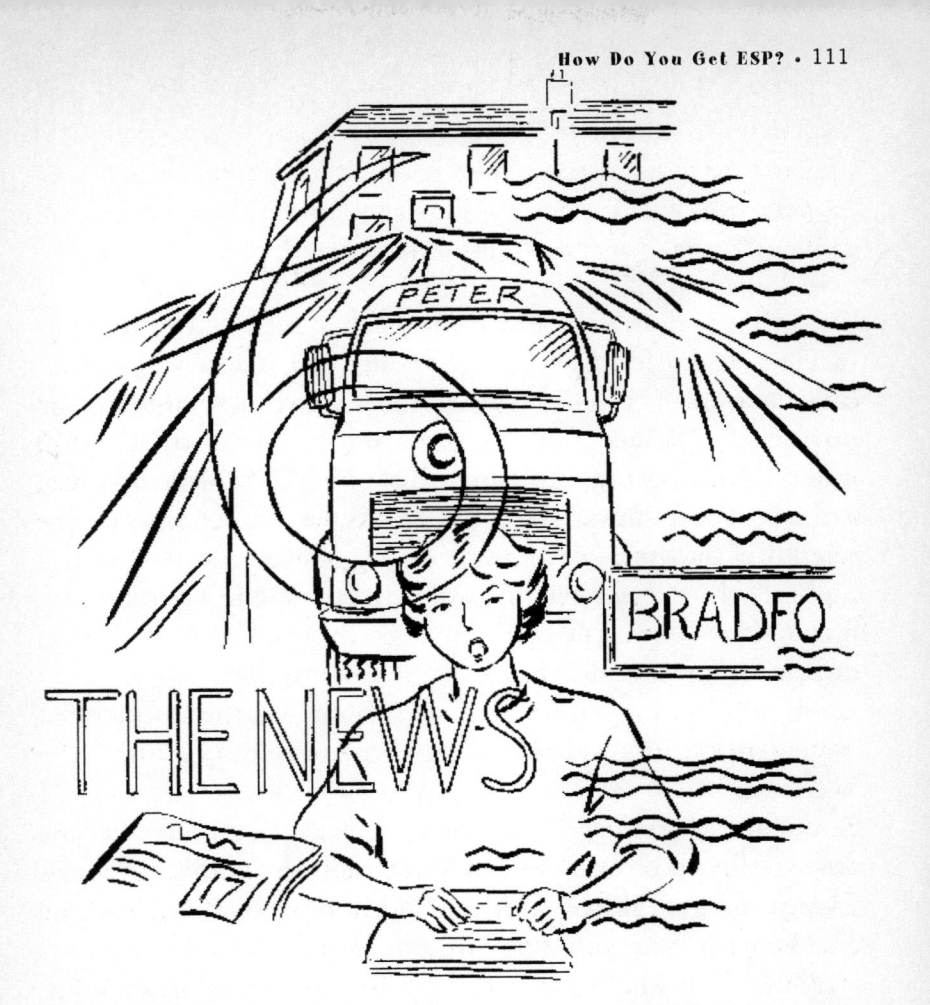

The next day, she told Shirley about what had happened, and Shirley was determined that Nella should go to the police with her story. So they went together. Unfortunately, the investigation had taken so many years that the paperwork was immense. This was just before the British police started to use computers, and all their information was kept on cards that were filed in a massive index system. And that includes the information that Nella gave them.

Peter Sutcliffe, the man they called the Yorkshire Ripper, was arrested on January 2, 1981. He was actually arrested for another offence — something that had happened to him once before during the investigation — but the arresting officers soon found weapons in his car and realized who they had on their hands.

And what about Nella's predictions? Well, his name was Peter. He was a truck driver from Bradford. He lived in a house that was on a hill — its street number was six. The company he worked for had their name on the doors of all their trucks: it was T.W. & H. Clark (Holdings) Ltd. With a capital "C".

But the worst aspect for Nella was that he had killed his last victim on November 17. Something she might have been able to prevent if her evidence hadn't been lost. But perhaps she shouldn't have felt so bad about this: after all, if it was possible that she was seeing a future news report leaking through time on her TV, then there was nothing she could do to prevent the murder taking place.

It was interesting that the image should appear on the television, though, as some psychics have been compared to badly tuned televisions.

The Dutchman With Strange Reception

Gerald Croiset was a Dutch psychic, just like Peter Hurkos. But the two men couldn't have been more different. Peter was a flamboyant man who loved working on the stage, and was even more pleased with the attention he got from television and the other media after he went to America. He stayed in America for many years, making it his home, and worked for many police forces as well as being the subject of a number of experiments by researchers at universities and US government laboratories. He even appeared in court at some trials to give evidence based on what he had "seen" either through psychometry or in a trance. Like Nella Jones, he was able to supply evidence to catch a killer who was terrorizing a university campus, killing young women. Unlike the way in which Nella's evidence was lost, Peter's evidence was very much in the forefront of the police investigation.

A citizen's group in Michigan called Hurkos after several female students at Michigan State University were murdered. When he arrived, he asked if the police could supply maps of the areas where the bodies had been found. Looking at them, he found that the roads running between the locations acted like mental triggers: he could see images running along them, as if he were watching a movie.

He described a man in his mid-twenties who was attending classes at the university in the evenings. He had a motorbike, and was thin but muscular. Peter saw the farmhouse location where police believed the killer had taken his victims (which surprised the policemen, as this was something they were keeping secret).

The description and the motorbike were clues that the police did not have. Using these, they were able to discover a common link between the girls – a man called Norman John Collins, who was later caught just after the death of his last victim. A death that Peter had seen, and knew he was powerless to stop.

The fact that many people with ESP haven't been able to use their powers to stop such things when they have been called in to help is a great worry to many of them. Does this mean that everything that will happen is already known? Or does it simply mean that these psychics can see part of the things that might happen (as we discussed earlier in some of the theories about ESP and time)?

The knowledge that, despite their powers, they haven't been able to prevent deaths makes some of them depressed. One such psychic was Gerald Croiset.

Croiset was once described by a writer as being like a badly tuned TV set. It seemed that his psychic visions came to him through a haze of fuzz and snow, rather like what happens when you press the random tuning button on a TV and it flicks through the static, finding a channel but not staying on it long enough for you to make any real sense of what's on the screen.

Gerald Croiset was a strange mixture of a man: although he was very flamboyant when alone in a room with two or three people, he didn't like the glare of mass attention. He helped the police from his home in Utrecht, where he had a small office and consulting room. His mother also had the gift of ESP.

Like Hurkos, Croiset was most successful with ESP if he used psychometry or dowsing over maps. A journalist called Frank Ryan once approached Croiset three years after the disappearance of a young woman called Pat McAdam. Pat had last been seen hitch-hiking on her way back to her Glasgow home.

Using a Bible that had belonged to the girl, and a map of

the area where she was last seen, Croiset concentrated very hard and appeared to go into a trance. Very slowly and carefully he described an area of woodland leading down to a stream. He described a bridge and a burned-out wreck of a car that was lying in a field. He believed that Pat had passed these and met with an accident that had resulted in her being swept down the river and out to sea.

Ryan returned to Scotland and went to the location Croiset had described. Sure enough, there was the bridge and the burned-out car. There was also a scrap of dress material, torn off some time before by the look of it, that had been trapped in some bushes. The material was never identified, and Pat was never found.

Five years later, in 1976, Croiset was flown to the location by a BBC-TV film crew. It was the first time he had seen the site and, although Pat's body has never been found, Croiset was sure that what he had described was the truth.

Croiset was half-Jewish and, like Peter Hurkos, had worked with the resistance during World War II. He also spent time in internment camps because of his Jewish heritage. While in these camps, he was able to see which of the people around him would die, and this aspect of his gift haunted him forever. He was a nervous, highly-strung man, and suffered from stress-related stomach complaints all his life.

Although he never travelled abroad, he was once able to help New York police find a missing girl from a series of maps he studied while sitting at home in Utrecht. Four-year-old Edith Kiecorius had gone missing in New York City. A small girl answering her description was seen boarding a plane at the airport with a woman who wasn't – according to her passport – her mother. The New York police knew she was bound for San Francisco, and they asked Croiset to help find her, offering to fly him over.

He refused, and asked only for maps of New York and San Francisco. When he received them, he dowsed and studied them carefully. The police were not pleased when he told them that the girl was still in New York. He even gave them a street location and a description of the MAN who had kidnaped her.

The police dismissed him as being of no use – until they caught up with the woman and small girl, and found that she wasn't Edith, and that the woman with her was her aunt. Only then did they turn their attention to what Croiset had told them, and found Edith within a couple of days, held in a one-room apartment.

Once again, the badly tuned television set that was Croiset's brain had managed to catch a station for a few seconds – a station marked New York – just long enough for the psychic to see what was on the channel.

Although Croiset was called the badly tuned TV, the same could also be said of Peter Hurkos, or Nella Jones – or even Uri Geller. It seems that ESP is something that many people can achieve to a degree, but which we are not really ready for yet. Perhaps those people who believe that ESP powers are the next step in humanity's evolution are right, and the people who have these powers right now are the beginnings of that next jump in humankind's development.

QUESTIONS

◆▸ As Pat McAdam was never found, how could Gerald Croiset have been so sure that he had the answer to her disappearance?

- ◆✦ Both Peter Hurkos and Gerald Croiset were able to give the police information simply by looking at maps. Do you think this was dowsing or psychometry of some kind, or do you think they were able to guess things from other information they had been given?

- ◆✦ Speaking of information – some scientists describe the world that we can't see "the information universe," and claim that our brains filter out everything we don't need for everyday use. Do you think that some part of the brain could use such things as maps as triggers to unlock part of that universe?

SOME TESTS BEFORE THE END!

So here we are near the end of this book, and although there have been lots of questions, it's been a while since we had some tests. Here are three that test your precognition and can be done at any time.

- ◆✦ When you're out, see if you can tell what sort of car will next come round the corner – will it be a small blue one, a large silver one, a Pontiac, a Ford, etc. You could even guess how many people will be in it, and whether it will be driven by a man or a woman. Make a note of your results and how often you are correct or even partially correct.

- ◆✦ If you're waiting for a bus, ask yourself how long it will take to arrive, and then time it. Make a note of how close you are to being correct.

◆✦ If the phone rings when you're at home, see if you can tell who's calling before you answer. If you're phoning someone else, see if you know whether or not they'll be at home, or who will answer the phone (Mum, Dad, your friend, Aunt Flo, whoever). Again, make a note of your results.

Remember that statistics – odds and numbers – decide if you have more ESP potential than the norm. So keep a careful eye on those results!

CHAPTER 7

Yes, But What Can You Do With It?

And now we're at the last part of the book, so this is a very good question. What can you do with any ESP powers you might have?

In terms of helping people, you might already have gathered that the fact of ESP being very erratic means that you can't guarantee that you're going to get something right – what some psychics call a "hit." Which makes it a very tricky business if you want to do things like work with the police. If you get something wrong, you're called a fake. And even if you get it right, that's no guarantee that anyone is going to believe in your ESP.

In the UK, the police do not, officially, believe in psychics or ESP. Of course, people like Nella Jones and Chris

Robinson work for the police, but this is usually at the request of individual officers who have had some experience of them in the past.

In the USA, some police forces have a policy of using psychics in cases where there seems to be no way in which the evidence links together and they're totally baffled. In fact, the University of California has a database of psychics who have worked with different police forces and have obtained a positive result.

But the problem is that many people think they have ESP when they don't. And a lot of people know they don't but see a way of pretending that they do and making money out of selling their story to the media. This makes the police very wary of anyone who approaches them. In fact, it makes anyone feel extremely suspicious if approached by a person who claims to have ESP.

If you want to earn money from ESP, then it is possible: but as a career option, you'd be much better off trying to be a professional footballer or a pop star. Because any ESP powers you may have tend to come and go as they please, and can't be relied upon. This makes people very reluctant to give you money.

But supposing you could get around this, and you had ESP. What could you do?

Finding Missing People

This usually means working with the police, although a lot of psychics are approached by the families of people who are missing. There isn't a lot of money in this directly – if you can't find the person, or they turn up dead, then the family won't pay you. And the police don't really pay anything more than your travel expenses – if that!

Anyway, setting yourself up as a psychic detective won't do you a lot of good unless you already have some sort of reputation. People like the American psychics Greta Alexander and Dixie Yeterian have become famous because they are good at finding missing people – but this only started in each woman's case when she was asked by a family friend to help out in some way. From there it just snowballed as newspapers and TV got hold of the story.

This sort of thing takes the psychic into the realms of ...

Showbusiness

This is the big one. A psychic can make money in showbusiness, but it can bring BIG problems.

Nella Jones used to tour concert halls, as did Estelle Roberts, answering questions from people in the audience about problems they had, or dead relatives they wanted to talk to once again. Because they were good, they were then asked to write books. Doris Stokes and Doris Collins, who were both basically clairaudient, wrote lots of books, and appeared on television.

In the early 1970s, when I was a boy, I remember a TV show called *The Amazing Kreskin*, an American show where Jim Kreskin would read people's minds, bend metal, and do amazing tricks using the powers of his mind. It was very popular for a couple of years. Before TV, such psychics would appear in variety shows doing mind-reading acts.

BUT – and it's a very big but – if you're in showbusiness you have to get it right all the time or people call you a fake. For example, when Uri Geller appeared on the *Tonight* show and couldn't get his power to work, he was condemned as a fraud. But this was just one night. The next night, on another show, things worked fine. Too late – reports calling him a fake had already appeared.

The clairaudient Doris Stokes sometimes had people in her audiences who had rehearsed stories with her, so that even if her powers deserted her she would be able to put on some kind of show. Mind-readers evolve codes with their assistants so that they can always be sure of getting something right.

And then people who are paid to be skeptical come along and call you a cheat. And if you don't always get it right then they say you're a cheat because you can't always get a "hit."

So, although showbusiness can make you a lot of money, it's also tough if your powers are erratic, as most people with ESP find.

But why are they like this? Remember Uri Geller's theory on why he had trouble working with the FBI? The threat of people wanting to kill him because he was working with the police stressed him so much that the part of his brain that supplied his ESP couldn't break through into his conscious mind any more. The same thing applies to the stress of always having to be right. If this amount of pressure is put on you, then your brain seems to rebel.

The fact is that if ESP is the next step in our evolution, then we who are alive now haven't quite got there yet. Until we have, then the ESP won't flow smoothly. The likelihood is that science will only be able to explain it all when we have full ESP – by which time it won't need explaining any longer!

So what other career options are open to you?

Dowsing

This can be very lucrative if you know the right people. Uri Geller has made a fortune by dowsing for minerals, and taking a very small percentage of the revenue of what is found instead of receiving a fee. But he was only able to do this because of the name he had made for himself – without being famous he would never have met his first industrialist. In fact, if you or I turned up at the reception desk of a mining company with maps and a pendulum saying we could find minerals by dowsing, unless they knew who we were it's likely that we'd be shown the door by a security guard pretty quickly!

So, if you have to be famous to be a big mineral dowser, then what else can you do?

Dowse for water. These days, with the greenhouse effect and the long, hot summers leading to water shortages at certain times of the year, it becomes more important for people to find hidden springs and wells. In the last few years, a lot of farmers have employed dowsers to find water on their land.

But this is only once a year, and the pay isn't that great.

If you were really good at dowsing, you could hire yourself out to do such things as dowse to see whether a pregnant woman is going to have a boy or girl – but an ultrasound scan may tell her that anyway.

I guess it's not that easy to make money with ESP. Maybe that's just as well. It does seem that people who deliberately try to make money with their ESP end up losing some of their powers, at least temporarily. So that just leaves one thing …

Working For The Government

This is a bit of a spooky one. Just as in *The X Files*, there are secret government projects in which ESP is used. The most famous one was the US Government's remote viewing project, which had the code-name Stargate. It began in 1973 at the Stanford Research Institute in California, when members of the army and navy who had shown degrees of ESP were studied by scientists and coached by psychics until they were able to "see" things on the other side of the world.

Sitting in a room, with only a set of map co-ordinates, the members of Stargate were able to concentrate and view images from the other side of the world. One member recalled going into a bunker in Soviet Russia, before the Iron Curtain between the East and West collapsed, and seeing a man who was being held prisoner. As it was a military operation, these psychics were used as spies, finding the location and lay-out of enemy airfields and missile sites. So some people were ESP spies!

But the project was disbanded in 1995, and if there is anything like it still in operation, then it's VERY, VERY secret. And you can't apply for a job there – you have to be taken down a dark alleyway and told you're going to be doing it, with lots of secret code-words.

So that's that.

Conclusion

Even if you only set yourself up finding lost dogs in the neighborhood for a tiny fee, you've still got to get it right all the time otherwise people will ask for their money back and tell everyone how useless you are.

We might as well face the fact that making money from ESP is not likely unless you do something amazing by accident, and it all happens by chance.

Really, the only thing to do is to work on developing any powers you might have, and to enjoy having them and exploring your mind. If you push them too hard, they'll go away.

And that would really spoil the fun!